CHEF PAUL PRUDHOMME'S

KITCHEN EXPEDITION

Photographs by

Paul Rico

Art by

Harrel Gray

Published by Paul Prudhomme Foods
New Orleans, Louisiana

Library of Congress Cataloging-in-Publication Data
Prudhomme, Paul
Chef Paul Prudhomme's Kitchen Expedition / Paul Prudhomme
p.   cm.
ISBN 0-9656348-0-9
1. Cookery, American. 2. Cookery (Herbs) 3. Spices. I. Title.
1997

Printed in Canada

First Edition

Also by Chef Paul Prudhomme

Chef Paul Prudhomme's Louisiana Kitchen
The Prudhomme Family Cookbook
  (with the Prudhomme Family)
Chef Paul Prudhomme's Seasoned America
Chef Paul Prudhomme's Fork in the Road
Chef Paul Prudhomme's Pure Magic
Chef Paul Prudhomme's Fiery Foods That I Love

Table of Contents

Introduction

Hi! Let's get started on our Kitchen Expedition!

I've probably said a hundred times—no, maybe a thousand—that my goal in life is to make your dinner better. Every dish I create, every recipe I write, is done with that in mind, so as I travel around the city and around the world I'm constantly trying new tastes and learning different ways of preparing food. I frequently arrange to take cooking lessons, especially from cooks in other countries. Even though my instructors are professional chefs, what I ask them for is information on their traditional, native dishes, the kinds of foods they eat at home for regular family meals or special occasions. Usually, however, the first thing they want to show me is how talented and professional they are, by preparing the most elegant and complicated dishes they can come up with! This is great, but not what I have in mind, so I always explain again, and for the second class they show me what I really want to see. And taste. It's from these simpler, more traditional dishes that I get some really great ideas to share with you.

I never actually write recipes or anything down; I try to remember tastes, and it's those memories I call up when I get home to the test kitchen. With the able assistance of Sean O'Meara, a computer expert who loves to cook and eat, and Chef Crispin Pasia, whom I met when he was executive sous chef at the Hong Kong Marriott, I begin to play with these tastes and the ideas they inspire to adapt them for your kitchen. I say "play," for although it's my work, I enjoy it so much it seems like fun to me.

Anyway, in the test kitchen I use these combinations and methods to create new dishes that I love. You know I have to *really love* a dish before I'm going to put it into a cook book, because I don't see any point in introducing an ingredient simply for the sake of presenting something new. The dish has got to be the very best I can make it, and it's got to have a complexity, a depth of flavor that's exciting and that holds my (and therefore your) interest from the first bite to the last.

Many times the end result of this work will look like a traditional recipe, such as gumbo or egg rolls or stew, but you can be sure it will have some unusual little twist in the ingredients or method that sets it apart from anything I've done myself or even tasted before. If a recipe doesn't have that special, new touch, or if we don't think it's the best possible dish of its kind, then, in spite of all the work Sean and Chris and I may have done, we toss it. Good is not good enough—it's got to be great! I think all these recipes are great! Each one has some special attribute that warrants its inclusion in the book. In the notes that accompany each recipe we give you information about the ingredients, or the combinations, or the method, and we've tried to explain everything so clearly that you'll feel as though I'm right there in your kitchen with you.

As you probably know, we've produced a series for public television stations using the recipes in this book—look for it on your local PBS channel. When we taped these programs, we tried to work as though you were right there in the studio kitchen with us. I hope you've noticed that I'm talking to you, not to some other person on camera with me, because *you* are the one for whom I'm demonstrating the recipes. We must be doing this right, because apparently a lot of you forget that the series is taped; many times when I travel people will come up to me and ask something like "How can you be here (in whatever city) today, when you're going to be on TV tomorrow?" That kind of response makes me feel really good, because it tells me each segment is so real to you that you feel like it's being broadcast live, rather than taped.

But taped it is, and believe me, it's a complicated production! It takes many people performing a wide variety of tasks to make it work, and much of the effort is expended before we ever set foot in the studio. Shawn Granger McBride, the president and chief executive officer of Magic Seasoning Blends, and Marty Cosgrove, Magic Seasoning Blends' executive chef, and I sit down and decide on the combination of recipes for each program. Usually we do three dishes, and we try to choose recipes that complement each other, yet use entirely different ingredients. Many times, but we're not compulsive about this, these are dishes that you could serve together.

While my staff and I are doing our planning, the crews at the television studio (WYES, Channel 12, the public television station in New Orleans) are busy building, decorating, and lighting the set. We've used a different set for each of my three TV series, and each one is even better than the previous one.

The day before taping, Marty shops for ingredients. Then he, Troy Brocato, one of my great-nephews and a whiz in the kitchen, and usually the kitchen staff of my restaurant, K-Paul's Louisiana Kitchen, "prep" them. Let's face it, watching me dice bell peppers on television would be about as interesting as grass growing, so all that is done beforehand.

Thank goodness for video editing, because without it we'd never be able to show you three recipes in a 30-minute program! We prepare the recipe completely once or twice, in addition to whatever I do on camera, so you'll be able to see how it'll look when it's completed. I don't work from a script, but we do write up a list of points I want to make about each dish, whether it's about some of the ingredients, or the method, or maybe where I got the idea. These are put on the TelePrompTer, just under the camera lens, so I can see them while I'm talking directly to you. Speaking of cameras, we always use three—one overhead and another two for straight-on shots—making it possible for you to view the preparation from all angles.

Finally the taping begins! If everything goes well we can do one show—three recipes—in a morning, and another show in the afternoon. You can see that an entire series of 26 programs takes at least 13 working days, but we like to factor in a couple of extra days to cover ourselves when stuff happens, as it generally does.

You might think this is the end of the project, but the editing is the most time-consuming work—finding the best of the hundreds of hours of videotape and forming them into an entertaining, informative, and smoothly running series of programs. This is an incredibly difficult task, taking a lot longer than the original taping, and I think the people at WYES do a terrific job.

Meanwhile my book editor, Patricia Kennedy Livingston, is busy getting all the recipes organized and making them as easy to understand as possible. We double check to be sure the ingredients are listed in the order they're used, and we try to tell you what to look for in the pot while you're cooking. After careful readings, Sean does the typesetting on his computer, and we ship the manuscript off to the printer.

The book wouldn't be complete, however, without Paul Rico's wonderful photographs. We've worked with Paul several times, and he always produces pictures that make you want to head straight for the kitchen. The evocative cover painting by our talented artist, Harrel Gray, adds immeasurably to the visual impact.

I hope now you understand a little of how the ideas, talents, dedication, and just plain hard work of a lot of people have all come together to make up this book. From the original idea that came to me, perhaps in a foreign country or my own back yard, through the development in the test kitchen, testing in Patricia's home kitchen and refining for presentation in the television studio, then production of the book itself, much love and labor have combined to produce these dishes.

So come along with me—let's take a discovery trip to explore new foods and seasonings and new ways of using them. Let's enjoy our Kitchen Expedition!

Good cooking,

Good eating,

Good loving,

List of Photographs

Notes from the Test Kitchen

Any motivated cook, beginner or experienced, can easily prepare all the recipes in this book, but there is a lot of information that can make the process even easier and the end result even better. Because these notes are too long to include on every page where they're applicable, and because they apply to so many of the recipes, we include them here at the beginning of the book. We hope that you'll browse through these first pages before you choose a recipe to try, and refer back to them as you cook. Before you know it, all this information will become an integral part of your culinary knowledge!

Chile Peppers are essential to almost all the recipes in this book! We use them fresh and we use them dried and ground, and we may roast either the fresh or the dried ones. We almost always use a combination of varieties, especially the ground chiles, to give the dish a rounded, balanced flavor.

The dried peppers you'll encounter most often in this book are Anaheim, New Mexico, árbol, ancho, chipotle, guajillo, and pasilla. With the exception of chipotle, whose smoky aroma and flavor are distinctive, you can use these interchangeably, depending upon what varieties are available. Now that is not to say that all these varieties taste alike, for they all have distinct flavors, and each one drives the flavor of the dish in a different way. I suggest you make an effort to find the various peppers and become familiar with their differences. It will be an adventure for you to experiment, and as you learn more about chiles you'll want to use the specific ones listed in the ingredients or the ones you like best. If you demand a variety of chiles—fresh or dried—from your grocer, chances are he'll be able to supply you.

However you probably won't be able to buy these peppers already ground, even when you can buy them dried. If that's the case, simply grind them yourself (an inexpensive coffee grinder works well), and store them in clearly labeled, tightly closed glass jars. If they're not crisp enough to grind easily, dry them out on a cookie sheet in a 200° oven for 15 minutes, then cool and grind. See page 4 for instructions on roasting fresh chiles.

Among the fresh chile peppers we like to use are jalapeño, serrano and bird's eye peppers. All chiles vary greatly in amount of capsicum oil (the hot stuff!) they contain, and both wax peppers and poblano chiles are so mild they are closer to bell peppers than other chile peppers.

If you handle peppers with your hands, then rub your eyes it's likely to burn a lot, and some people even find peppers burn their skin. The best way to avoid pain and suffering is to wear thin latex or plastic gloves—we get disposable ones from the pharmacy—and throw them away after use. They'll slip on and off easily, even on a humid day, if ~~you sprinkle co~~ ᵑn your hands first. A clean old spice jar with a shaker lid makes a perfect container for the corn starch. Be sure to wash the cutting board and knives in hot soapy water after use.

Because chile peppers are becoming more and more popular, you probably will be able to find fresh and dried ones in your neighborhood supermarket, and if your community boasts ethnic or international markets, you'll no doubt be able to choose from a wide variety. My company, Magic Seasoning Blends, offers a selection of ground, dried chiles by mail. These are the same ones we used to test the recipes in this book. To place an order or obtain a catalog, write or call:

Chef Paul Prudhomme's Magic Seasoning Blends®
824 Distributors Row
New Orleans LA 70123
(504) 731-3590
(800) 457-2857

Cook over high heat is an instruction you'll find in most of my recipes. When you brown vegetables really fast, you caramelize them, bringing out a dark sweet flavor that enriches your dish and gives it depth. High heat on your stove may be a different temperature than it is on mine, and different pots and pans transfer heat differently, so use your good judgment. Generally, the heavier the pot, the higher the heat you can use. This kind of cooking is not something you can go off and leave—you have to watch it. If the food looks like it's just about to burn, for goodness' sake turn the heat down, or remove it from the heat until it's cool, then return it to a lower heat.

The times we list are just to serve as guides, except for cases in which the food is very liquid. Most of the time we try to describe how the food should look at a critical stage, so it's more important to watch, smell, and taste the food than to follow the number of minutes slavishly. And I strongly suggest adding your own notes—about pots, times, or any other hints—right on the recipe, so the next time you cook it you'll know what worked best for you. After all, a cookbook is meant to be used, not placed on a shelf and admired.

Julienne is the term for cutting vegetables—such as bell peppers, onions or carrots—into long, thin pieces. The size we use most often is about 2½ inches long by ¼ inch wide and thick.

Olive oil adds its distinctive flavor to your dish, unlike blander oils we generally use for frying, so it's vital that you like the taste of the oil you're using. Many people are attracted to Extra Virgin olive oils, which are usually a green color and have a strong flavor, whereas in most of my cooking, I prefer to use olive oil bottled by James Plagnoil in Marseille, France. It definitely tastes like olive oil, which is what I want, but it doesn't overpower the other flavors. This is a personal choice, and you should taste several varieties, perhaps choosing two or three different types for different purposes. I think it's a lot of fun to experiment!

Some olive oils can be super expensive. When you start using them you should buy a variety of oils, and use the one you like, without regard to price. If you like the taste in the bottle, you'll love it in your food.

An ounce is not always an ounce! Some ounces measure weight, such as 16 ounces equal a pound (handy for sugar, flour, cereal, beans, etc.), and other ounces measure liquid or volume, such as 8 ounces equal one cup (soup, juice, ketchup, etc.). Normally we don't have a problem with this quirky vestige of Medieval measurement—we don't even think about buying sugar by the pound and using it by the cup. But then we begin to talk about dairy products. Milk and cream are sold by volume, for example pints (2 cups or 16 ounces), quarts, and gallons. On the other hand, yogurt, sour cream and cream cheese are sold by weight, so that in these cases, "8 ounces " indicates ½ pound, not one cup. Therefore, when you see yogurt, sour cream, or cream cheese in one of my recipes, and it's measured in cups, don't assume that an 8-ounce package will measure one cup. Eight ounces of water by weight will equal one cup or eight fluid ounces, and perhaps that's what all this ounce/ounce mess was originally based on, but most substances don't weigh the same number of ounces that they measure by volume.

Roasting vegetables, such as onions, garlic, bell peppers, and chile peppers, is a technique that we use in several recipes to add a smoky, roasted, nutty, fabulous, emotional taste you can't get any other way.

If your stove is gas, simply place the vegetables right in the flame, and turn them with tongs until the outer skin is black and charred all over. Immediately plunge into ice water, then rub off the black skin under running water. If there are stubborn spots that don't come off immediately, a sharp knife will take care of them. If your range is electric, you can roast vegetables in a preheated 500° oven. With either method, watch the peppers closely—there's a big difference between roasted and burned beyond recognition—you want to char just the thin outer skin.

Scalloping is a technique of slicing meat, usually flank steak, into ovals about 2 by 3 inches, so that the meat absorbs as much of the flavor of the seasoning mix as possible and cooks quickly. It's not hard to do; read the directions a couple of times, study the illustration as you do so and imagine how you'll hold the knife, and with a little practice you'll learn the technique in no time.

Start with the meat in front of you on a firm surface with the grain running from left to right. With a very sharp knife, make the first cut about 3 inches from the narrow end of the steak, beginning about 2 inches from one long side of the meat, slicing toward the end of the steak, through the thickness of the meat at an angle, so that you make a thin, wedge-shaped piece of meat about 3 inches long and 2 inches wide. The thicker end of this little piece should be not much more than ¼ inch thick, and it should taper off to almost nothing at the other end. You'll be cutting through the grain (which is very prominent in flank steak, the cut we recommend for scalloping) at an oblique angle, so you'll see short, white bits of stringy material, which simply holds the delicious fleshy meat together. From the top of the steak this material really does look almost like strings, and if you cut straight down through the meat, these "strings" would look more like little dots. In the same way make another wedge-shaped "scallop" right next to the first one, continuing across the width of the meat for the first row, then down the length of the meat until you've cut all the meat. Take your time and try to keep all the pieces as close to the same size as possible so they'll cook in the same amount of time.

Shrimp count is simply the number of shrimp per pound, an easy and fairly uniform way to indicate size. For example, 41 to 50 count shrimp, or 41 to 50 shrimp in each pound, would be very small, while 21 to 25 count shrimp would be twice as large, as only 21 to 25 shrimp would weigh a pound.

Stock would be the title of my theme song if I had one! At least 99% of my dishes are cooked with stock rather than water (which is terrific for washing dishes), and stock is so easy to make that I hope you'll follow my example.

You can make stock in any pot that is large enough to hold all the ingredients, but it's easiest in a stock pot, which is taller than it is wide. This shape means the liquid will have less surface in proportion to its volume than it does in a wider pot, so will evaporate more slowly, yet the stock will cook well and the flavors will be nicely concentrated. In addition to the vegetables mentioned below, you can use just about any in your kitchen, except bell peppers, which might make the stock spoil faster. And never add salt, herbs or spices to stock., because you don't want to interfere with the Seasoning Mix in the recipe you're getting ready to cook.

Vegetable Stock

2 quarts cool water
Vegetable trimmings from recipe
  you're cooking, if available
1 unpeeled medium-size onion,
  quartered

1 rib celery with leafy top,
  quartered
1 unpeeled large garlic clove,
  quartered

Place all the ingredients in a large stock pot over high heat and bring to a boil. Reduce the heat and simmer, adding water only as the liquid falls below 1 quart. Cook the stock for 8 hours or even overnight if possible, but if not, as long as you can—even stock simmered for as little as 30 minutes is better than water. Makes 1 quart.

Chicken Stock

Back, neck and giblets (except
  liver) from chicken you're
  cooking (or buy chicken wings or
  other inexpensive parts)
2 quarts cool water
Vegetable trimmings from recipe
  you're cooking, if available

1 unpeeled medium-size onion,
  quartered
1 rib celery with leafy top,
  quartered
1 unpeeled large garlic clove,
  quartered

Roast the chicken pieces in a 350° oven until they're golden brown, about 20 to 30 minutes, depending on the size. Place all the ingredients in a large stock pot over high heat and bring to a boil. Reduce the heat and simmer, adding water only as the liquid falls below 1 quart. Cook the stock for 8 hours or even overnight if possible, but if not, as long as you can—even stock simmered for as little as 30 minutes is better than water. Makes 1 quart.

Meat Stock

Bones and scraps from the recipe
   or ½ pound soup meat and bone
2 quarts cool water
Vegetable trimmings from recipe
   you're cooking, if available

1 unpeeled medium-size onion,
   quartered
1 rib celery with leafy top,
   quartered
1 unpeeled large garlic clove,
   quartered

Roast the bones and meat in a 350° oven, turning once, until they're nicely browned, about 30 minutes. Place all the ingredients in a large stock pot over high heat and bring to a boil. Reduce the heat and simmer, adding water only as the liquid falls below 1 quart. Cook the stock for 8 hours or even overnight if possible, but if not, as long as you can—even stock simmered for as little as 30 minutes is better than water. Makes 1 quart.

Seafood or Fish Stock

2 quarts cool water
Vegetable trimmings from recipe
   you're cooking, if available
1 unpeeled medium-size onion,
   quartered
1 rib celery with leafy top,
   quartered

1 unpeeled large garlic clove,
   quartered
Shrimp, crawfish, or crab shells,
   or fish trimmings from the
   recipe, if available, or purchase
   a small amount

Place all the ingredients in a large stock pot over high heat and bring to a boil. Reduce the heat and simmer, adding water only as the liquid falls below 1 quart. Cook the stock for 8 hours or even overnight if possible, but if not, as long as you can—even stock simmered for as little as 30 minutes is better than water. Makes 1 quart.

*   *   *

Strain the stock through several layers of cheesecloth before using. These recipes can be doubled or tripled if your stock pot is big enough. You can keep leftover stock for several days in the refrigerator, or freeze it for future use. If you reduce your stock, it will take up even less storage space. To reduce stock, after straining it, pour it into a clean stock pot and bring it back to a boil over high heat. As soon as it boils, lower the heat and simmer the stock until it is reduced to the desired level. This produces a very rich stock that can be used as is, or, if you don't want stock with so concentrated a flavor, dilute it before you use it. After cooling the stock, refrigerate or freeze it. Here's a handy idea: freeze the reduced stock in ice cube trays, then wrap each individual cube before returning to the freezer for storage. Label any container of stock that is to be refrigerated or frozen with the date and type of stock.

Toasting seeds, such as mustard, poppy or sunflower, gives them a wonderful rich flavor that adds depth to some of our recipes. It's easy to do—simple heat them in a heavy skillet over high heat, stirring or shaking the skillet constantly, until they brown slightly. Once they begin to heat up, they may start popping, which can be surprising if you're not expecting it and also causes you to lose some as they pop right out of the skillet, so you may need to lower the heat once this happens. Watch the seeds carefully, for you don't want to burn them.

Tomatoes add color, flavor, acidity, nutrition, and liquid to many of these recipes, and many times we specify fresh ones. If, however, the only tomatoes available when you're ready to cook are hard, pale and flavorless, you have my express permission to use good canned ones! In fact a number of these dishes were tested with canned tomatoes, because you can depend on their unvarying quality. We have found in the Test Kitchen that Hunt's® Choice-Cut™ Diced Tomatoes work well for us.

Here's an easy way to peel a fresh tomato: first, cut a shallow "x" on the end opposite the stem end. Next plunge the tomato into rapidly boiling water for about 1 minute, then, under cold running water, starting from the "x," just slip off the skin. Use your paring knife to remove any skin still adhering in the crevices of the stem end.

Zest is the outer, colorful skin of citrus fruits. We call for lemon or lime zest in some of these recipes, and you get it by using a zester, a special tool with several small, circular, sharp-edged holes. Pull the tool from one end of the fruit to the opposite, and firmly remove just the brightly colored outer skin. Be careful not to get any of the white pith beneath the colorful outer skin, for it's very bitter. Zest makes an attractive garnish for food or drinks, and may be used as is as an ingredient, or chopped if the recipe so specifies. An alternative to zest is grated peel, but here again avoid the white pith.

The journey of a thousand miles begins with but a single step.

... Old Chinese proverb

APPETIZERS

Fried Oysters and Magic Dipping Sauce

Photograph No. 1

MAKES 6 TO 8 APPETIZER SERVINGS

Everybody fries seafood, so you would be perfectly justified if you asked "What's so special about this recipe?" Well, I'll tell you—it's the unusual seasoning mix. The addition of dill seeds, thyme leaves and ancho peppers sets these oysters apart from any you've ever tasted before. Also, notice that we've used different seasonings for the oysters themselves and the dipping sauce, to make the flavor combination more complex, with the oregano and garlic powder to tie them together.

By the way, it's no longer true that you can eat oysters only in months with an "R" in them. That was sound advice in the years before good refrigeration and rapid transport, because they'd likely spoil in the heat. Now just be sure to buy the freshest oysters you can find.

A hint for successful deep-frying is never to let the oil's temperature drop much below 350°. The temperature may drop a little bit when you add the oysters (or whatever you're frying), but if it drops too much your fried food will be oily instead of crisp. If the temperature falls too much (25° or more), try frying smaller batches.

These wonderful oysters make a great meal all by themselves, or use them to make a traditional "Po' Boy" sandwich: slice a length of warm French bread, slather it with our Magic Dipping Sauce, then pile on the hot oysters. In New Orleans when we say our Po' Boy is "dressed," we mean it has thinly sliced tomatoes and shredded lettuce on it. Squeeze a lemon over the oysters and add mustard if you like. Delicious!

We've listed the sauce first, because you'll want to make it before you start frying so it'll be done the minute the oysters are ready.

Magic Dipping Sauce

MAKES ABOUT 1½ CUPS

1 cup mayonnaise
¼ cup ketchup
2 tablespoons Chef Paul
   Prudhomme's Magic Pepper
   Sauce®
1 tablespoon dark brown sugar
1 teaspoon onion powder

1 teaspoon oregano
1 teaspoon ground dried Anaheim
   chile peppers (see pages 1 and 2)
1 teaspoon ground dried ancho
   chile peppers (see pages 1 and 2)
½ teaspoon garlic powder

Combine all the ingredients thoroughly. Refrigerate any leftover sauce.

SEASONING MIX

2½ teaspoons dried oregano leaves
2½ teaspoons salt
2 teaspoons sweet basil leaves
2 teaspoons paprika
1¼ teaspoons dill seeds
1¼ teaspoons onion powder
1¼ teaspoons cayenne

1¼ teaspoons dried thyme leaves
1 teaspoon garlic powder
1 teaspoon black pepper
¾ teaspoon white pepper
¾ teaspoon ground dried ancho chile
   peppers (see pages 1 and 2)

4 dozen oysters, drained
1 cup corn flour (see page 167)
1 cup corn meal

1 cup all-purpose flour
8 cups vegetable oil

Combine the seasoning mix ingredients in a small bowl and mix well.

Season the oysters evenly with 2 tablespoons of the seasoning mix and refrigerate them for at least 1 hour.

Remove the oysters from the refrigerator 1 hour before using to prevent lowering the oil temperature too much when frying.

Thoroughly combine the corn flour, corn meal, all-purpose flour, and the remaining seasoning mix.

In a 6-quart pot, heat the oil to 350°, using a cooking thermometer and adjusting the heat as necessary to keep the oil as close to 350° as possible. If you have one, an electric skillet or an electric deep-fryer that has a thermostat will work well.

Before you start to fry, let me emphasize for best results, don't let the oysters sit in the coating mixture. Fry the oysters as soon as they are well coated! Now, place a handful of the oysters in the dry coating mixture. Cover them with a mound of the mixture and press down gently, coating them completely. Shake off the excess coating and immediately and very carefully drop them, one at a time, into the hot oil. Fry the oysters until they float in the oil and are golden brown. Drain on paper towels, and repeat the process, working in small batches, until all the oysters are fried. Serve immediately with our Magic Dipping Sauce.

Chicken Poppers and Simple Sauce

MAKES 8 APPETIZER SERVINGS OR 4 MAIN-COURSE SERVINGS

These are great as an appetizer, but some of my testers ate so many they didn't have room for dinner!

I think one reason for this recipe's great popularity is its unusual taste, thanks to the sage, ancho peppers, and pasilla peppers in the seasoning mix—it's really a different way to season chicken. It's also quick and easy to prepare, and look, the sauce is truly simple.

Simple Sauce

MAKES 1¼ CUPS

1 cup mayonnaise
¼ cup ketchup

1 tablespoon Chef Paul
    Prudhomme's Magic Pepper
    Sauce®

Make the sauce first, by combining all ingredients, so you'll have it ready when the chicken is fried. Refrigerate any leftover sauce.

SEASONING MIX

1½ teaspoons dried basil leaves
1½ teaspoons ground dried Anaheim
    chile peppers (see pages 1 and 2)
1½ teaspoons salt
1½ teaspoons dried thyme leaves
1 teaspoon garlic powder
1 teaspoon onion powder
1 teaspoon paprika

½ teaspoon cayenne
½ teaspoon black pepper
½ teaspoon white pepper
½ teaspoon ground sage
¼ teaspoon ground dried ancho chile
    peppers (see pages 1 and 2)
¼ teaspoon ground dried pasilla
    chile peppers (see pages 1 and 2)

1½ cups unseasoned bread crumbs
1 tablespoon dark brown sugar
1 tablespoon white balsamic
    vinegar (see page 172)
1 tablespoon prepared horseradish
1 tablespoon Worcestershire sauce
1 tablespoon Chef Paul
    Prudhomme's Magic Pepper
    Sauce®

1 teaspoon sesame oil
2 large eggs, lightly beaten
8 chicken breast halves (1½ to 2
    pounds total) sliced into ½-inch
    by 1½-inch strips
Vegetable oil for frying

Combine the seasoning mix ingredients in a small bowl and mix well, then combine 1 tablespoon plus 1 teaspoon of the seasoning mix with the bread crumbs in a cake pan and mix well. Set the seasoned bread crumbs aside.

The next step is to marinate the chicken. (A very easy way to do this is to use a strong plastic zipper bag and seal it tightly, but if you prefer you can use a bowl—just cover it with plastic wrap or foil while the chicken marinates.) Make a paste by combining the brown sugar, vinegar, horseradish, Worcestershire sauce, Magic Pepper Sauce, sesame oil, eggs, and the remaining seasoning mix. Mix the chicken strips in this paste and work them with your hands until they are evenly and thoroughly coated. Cover and let sit to soak up the flavors.

Now we're going to offer you a choice—regular or quick method. The regular method is to refrigerate the chicken overnight, then remove it from the refrigerator 1 hour before you're ready to fry it. The quick method is to let the chicken marinate for 1 hour (the vinegar in the marinade will keep it safe even without refrigeration for that time), then proceed with frying.

Pour enough vegetable oil into a large skillet to measure 2 inches deep and heat it to 350°, using a cooking thermometer and adjusting the heat as necessary to keep the oil as close to 350° as possible. If you have one, an electric skillet works very well.

Before you start to fry, let me emphasize for best results, don't let the chicken sit in the bread crumbs. Fry the strips as soon as they are coated! Now, lay as many pieces of chicken as will fit on top of half of the seasoned bread crumbs. Cover the chicken with the rest of the crumbs and press down gently, coating them completely. Shake off the excess crumbs and immediately and very carefully drop the chicken pieces into the hot oil. Fry the chicken until golden brown, remove with tongs, and drain on paper towels. Repeat the process, working in small batches, until all the strips are cooked. Serve with Simple Sauce.

Crab Meat and Sweet Potato Puddings

MAKES 6 TO 8 APPETIZERS

This dish was a hit with everyone who tried it! The texture is soft and creamy, almost like a quiche, and the little puddings come out of the oven brown and bubbly, just bursting with aroma and flavor. The basil, dill, and mustard are here to take the dish out of the dessert category—in Louisiana sweet potatoes are very often used as desserts, and I wanted to create something different. You can use 1½ cups of green bell peppers instead of all three colors, as sometimes the red and yellow ones are a little expensive. A low-fat alternative would be to make the recipe without the oil—just use a hot dry pan to cook the vegetables, and substitute low-fat sour cream for the cream and use low-fat or fat-free cheeses.

Seasoning Mix

2 teaspoons paprika
2 teaspoons salt
2 teaspoons dried basil leaves
1½ teaspoons dried dill weed
1½ teaspoons onion powder
1½ teaspoons dried oregano leaves

1 teaspoon garlic powder
1 teaspoon dry mustard
½ teaspoon cayenne
½ teaspoon black pepper
½ teaspoon white pepper

1 large or 2 small sweet potato(es), about ¾ pound total
½ cup heavy cream
2 tablespoons grated Parmesan cheese
2 tablespoons grated Romano cheese
1 tablespoon plus 2 teaspoons olive oil
1½ cups chopped onions, about 1 medium
½ cup chopped green bell peppers, about ½ medium
½ cup chopped red bell peppers, about ½ medium

½ cup chopped yellow bell peppers, about ½ medium
½ cup chopped celery, about 1 stalk
1½ cups crab stock, preferred, or seafood stock (see page 6), in all
2 teaspoons minced fresh garlic, about 2 cloves
½ pound lump crab meat, picked over to remove the shells and cartilage
1 cup freshly grated mozzarella cheese

Combine the seasoning mix ingredients in a small bowl and mix well.

Scrub the potato(es), and pierce three or four times with the tines of a fork to let the steam escape so it (they) will bake, not steam. Cook in a microwave on high heat, turning once or twice, until soft to the touch, about 7 minutes, depending on size. If you prefer, bake in a conventional oven, which will produce a sweeter, roasted taste. Peel the sweet potato(es) and place in an electric mixer along with the cream. At high speed, whip the potatoes and cream until the mixture is light and fluffy and the potatoes become lighter in color, about 5 minutes. Add the Parmesan and Romano cheeses, whip for 2 minutes longer, and set aside.

Preheat the oven to 350°.

In a large skillet over high heat, heat the oil just until it begins to smoke, about 3 to 4 minutes. Add the onions, all the bell peppers, the celery, and 1 tablespoon of the seasoning mix. Cook, stirring and scraping the bottom of the skillet every minute or two, for 5 minutes. Cover and cook, uncovering to stir and scrape every 3 minutes, until the vegetables lose their bright colors and begin to brown, about 6 or 7 minutes. Uncover and stir in ½ cup of the stock, 2 tablespoons of the seasoning mix, and the garlic. Cook, uncovered, whisking frequently, for 3 minutes—you'll see the vegetables are nicely browned now. Cook for 1½ minutes, stir in ½ cup stock, and cook for 2 more minutes. Stir in the remaining seasoning mix and the remaining ½ cup stock, and when they are thoroughly combined, add this mixture to the set-aside potato mixture still in the mixing bowl. Let cool to room temperature, then gently fold in the crab meat.

Divide the mixture among 6 to 8 (depending upon their size) ramekins or custard cups, and sprinkle about 2 tablespoons of mozzarella cheese on top of each one. Place the ramekins in a pan whose sides are higher than the ramekins. Add enough water to the pan to come about ¾ of the way up the sides of the ramekins.

Bake until the cheese is brown and bubbly, about 25 minutes. Use pot holders when you remove the pan from the oven, and be extremely careful, for the water is very hot! Using an oven mitt or pot holder, remove the ramekins from the water and place them briefly on a towel to drain. Serve immediately.

Crawfish and Cilantro Slats

Photograph No. 2

MAKES 12 SERVINGS

This wonderful appetizer can be made with shrimp instead of crawfish if you prefer—use a pound of 41 to 50 count (the number of shrimp in a pound), which will be just about the same size as crawfish. As the title suggests, the fresh cilantro is important to the flavor, so don't substitute. Flat parsley looks a lot like cilantro, but their aromas and flavors are entirely different. If you're not sure which is which, ask the produce manager. If you omit the crawfish (or shrimp) and use vegetable stock, you could serve this as a vegetarian dish, for there are enough vegetables to make a great stuffing, and the carefully balanced seasonings will take these slats anywhere you want to go!

Notice that in addition to the dried chile peppers, this recipe calls for fresh jalapeño and poblano chile peppers. To be sure you don't put too much heat into the dish, give the fresh peppers the taste test—snip off the tip and touch the cut part to your tongue. If just the touch is too hot for your tongue, you can be sure the whole pepper is going to be too hot for the dish, so use less or try another pepper. Serve with extra sour cream, plenty of guacamole, and our Pico de Gallo (page 44).

[Editor's note: We asked Chef Paul why these are called "slats," and he said that's because a slat is something you put under a thing to lift it, and here the tortillas actually support the fillings.]

SEASONING MIX

1¾ teaspoons ground cumin
1¾ teaspoons paprika
1¾ teaspoons salt
1 teaspoon dried basil leaves
1 teaspoon cayenne
1 teaspoon dried oregano leaves
1 teaspoon ground dried árbol chile peppers (see pages 1 and 2)

1 teaspoon dried thyme leaves
¾ teaspoon garlic powder
¾ teaspoon onion powder
½ teaspoon black pepper
½ teaspoon white pepper
½ teaspoon ground dried chipotle chile peppers (see pages 1 and 2)

2 tablespoons vegetable oil
1 cup chopped onions, about 1 small
½ cup chopped green bell peppers, about ½ medium
½ cup chopped red bell peppers, about ½ medium

½ cup chopped yellow bell peppers, about ½ medium
2 cups turnips, diced into ¼-inch cubes, about 1 large
½ cup fresh jalapeño chile peppers (see pages 1 and 2), diced into ¼-inch cubes

½ cup chopped poblano chile peppers, or other medium-to-mild variety (see pages 1 and 2)

1 tablespoon minced fresh garlic, about 3 cloves

½ cup seafood stock or vegetable stock (see page 6)

1 pound peeled crawfish tails with fat, or 1 pound 41/50 count peeled shrimp (see page 4)

12 (10-inch) flour tortillas

¾ cup sour cream (see page 3)

1 pound freshly grated Monterey Jack cheese

1 cup chopped green onions, about 12 stalks

2 cups loosely packed fresh cilantro leaves

3 tablespoons unsalted butter, melted

Combine the seasoning mix ingredients in a small bowl and mix well.

In a heavy 10-inch nonstick skillet over high heat, heat the oil just until it begins to smoke, about 3 to 4 minutes. Add the onions, bell peppers, and the turnips. Cook, stirring every 3 to 4 minutes, for 13 minutes, then add the jalapeños, poblanos (or other variety), garlic, and 4 tablespoons of the seasoning mix. Cook, stirring and scraping the bottom of the skillet thoroughly once a minute, for 3 minutes. Add the stock, scrape and stir well, then remove from the heat. Spread evenly on a sheet pan and refrigerate until chilled.

Season the crawfish (or shrimp) evenly with the remaining seasoning mix.

Preheat a 10-inch nonstick skillet over medium heat for 4 minutes.

Fold a tortilla in half, then open it up and spread 1 tablespoon sour cream evenly on one half of the tortilla, leaving an empty ½-inch border around the edge. Next, evenly spread ½ cup of the vegetable mixture over the sour cream, then add an even layer of crawfish tails (or shrimp), and top evenly with about 1 1/3 ounces of the grated cheese (about 1/12 of the total amount). Next sprinkle a generous tablespoon of the sliced green onions over the cheese, and top that layer with 2 tablespoons of cilantro. Re-fold the tortilla closed and brush one side with melted butter.

Place the filled tortilla, buttered side down, into the preheated skillet. Brush the top side with melted butter and weight it with a pot lid or small, heavy plate. Cook, turning once, until golden and crisp, about 2 to 3 minutes per side. Repeat with the remaining tortillas and fillings. To serve, cut each cooked filled tortilla into 3 wedges.

Marinated Artichokes

Photograph No. 1

MAKES 6 TO 8 SERVINGS

Buy artichokes that are dark green, heavy for their size, and have a tight leaf formation. And yes, there really are 24 cloves of garlic in this recipe! By the way, these artichokes taste even better the second day, and keep well under refrigeration.

SEASONING MIX

1½ teaspoons salt
1 teaspoon dill weed
1 teaspoon dry mustard
¾ teaspoon garlic powder
¾ teaspoon onion powder
¾ teaspoon dried oregano leaves
¾ teaspoon dried thyme leaves

½ teaspoon cayenne
½ teaspoon black pepper
½ teaspoon ground dried ancho chile peppers (see pages 1 and 2)
½ teaspoon ground dried chipotle chile peppers (see pages 1 and 2)
¼ teaspoon white pepper

24 baby artichokes
1 lemon, cut into ¼-inch slices
1 orange, cut into ¼-inch slices
2 cups chopped onions, about 1 large
3 cups celery root (see page 165), cut into julienne strips (see page 3), about 1 medium root

1 cup onions, cut into julienne strips (see page 3)
1 cup green bell peppers, cut into julienne strips (see page 3)
1 cup red bell peppers, cut into julienne strips (see page 3)
1 cup yellow bell peppers, cut into julienne strips (see page 3)
24 peeled garlic cloves

Lime and Orange Vinaigrette

½ cup fresh lime juice
¾ cup fresh orange juice
1 cup medium-dry sherry
4 tablespoons Chef Paul Prudhomme's Magic Pepper Sauce®
½ cup white balsamic vinegar (see page 172)

1 scant tablespoon lime zest (see page 7), about 3 limes
2 tablespoons fresh orange zest (see page 7), about 1 orange
2 tablespoons firmly packed light brown sugar

Combine the seasoning mix ingredients in a small bowl and mix well.

In a covered 4-quart pot over high heat, bring 3 quarts of water to a boil. Uncover and add the artichokes, lemon slices, orange slices, and chopped onions. Re-cover and return to a boil, uncover and add 2 tablespoons of the seasoning mix, the celery root, julienne onions, all the bell peppers, and the garlic. Boil, covered, for 15 minutes, then remove from the heat and let sit for 12 minutes.

Remove the artichokes from the water, and as soon as they are cool enough to handle, remove all the leaves from the stems, as well as the tough outer ones at the base of the bulbs. Snip off the prickly tips of the remaining leaves.

Combine the ingredients for the Lime and Orange Vinaigrette with the remaining seasoning mix. Process in a blender until well blended.

Drain the remaining vegetables (discarding the cooking liquid) and combine with the vinaigrette. Gently add the artichokes and refrigerate for at least 4 hours, preferably overnight, before serving.

Deep-Fried Wings with a Fresh Fennel Dipping Sauce

MAKES 4 SERVINGS

These wings have a wonderfully crunchy coating that offers a brand-new taste combination. The fresh fennel in the sauce adds the great taste of anise, which contrasts nicely with the peppers and sage and savory in the coating. By the way, if you can't find ground sage, substitute rubbed, and if you can't find ground savory, you can use the whole leaves, or grind them yourself in a coffee grinder.

Save the wing tips for making your stock—no point in letting them go to waste. Because the salinity of goat cheese varies, you may want to add a little salt to the dipping sauce—taste it and decide. Be sure the label indicates that it's pure goat cheese, for some companies add cow's milk to lower the cost. Among the brands I like to use are Silver Goat, Couturier, and Israeli Feta. By the way, I used less oil when I cooked these for the TV series, and called them "Pan-Fried." You can do them that way too if you prefer.

SEASONING MIX

1 tablespoon salt
2 teaspoons onion powder
1½ teaspoons cayenne
1½ teaspoons garlic powder
1½ teaspoons ground dried ancho
   chile peppers (see pages 1 and 2)

1½ teaspoons ground sage
1½ teaspoons ground savory
1 teaspoon black pepper
1 teaspoon white pepper
1 teaspoon ground dried pasilla chile
   peppers (see pages 1 and 2)

Sauce

2 large eggs
2 tablespoons fresh fennel leaves
   (just the feathery green parts
   that look like fresh dill), chopped

2 tablespoons honey
1½ cups vegetable oil
5 ounces firm, sharp goat cheese,
   crumbled

12 chicken wings, about 2 pounds
1 cup all-purpose flour
1 large egg, lightly beaten
1 cup milk

1 cup corn flour (see page 167)
1 cup corn meal
Vegetable oil, for frying

Combine the seasoning mix ingredients in a small bowl and mix well.

Make the sauce first, so it will be ready as soon as the wings are fried. In a blender combine the eggs, fennel leaves, honey, and 1 tablespoon of the seasoning mix. Process briefly to combine, then with the blender running, slowly add the oil in a thin stream. Transfer the mixture to a bowl and fold in the goat cheese.

Cut each wing into three sections at the joints, saving the tips for another purpose such as stock. Sprinkle the remaining 24 wing pieces evenly with 2 tablespoons of the seasoning mix, and rub it in well.

In a shallow pan, combine the all-purpose flour with 1 teaspoon of the seasoning mix and mix well. In a similar pan, combine the egg and milk and whisk until they are well blended. In a third pan, combine the corn flour, corn meal, and the remaining seasoning mix and stir until blended.

Pour enough vegetable oil into a large skillet to measure 2 inches deep, and heat it to 350°, using a cooking thermometer and adjusting the heat as necessary to keep the oil as close to 350° as possible. If you have one, an electric skillet works well.

Before you start to fry, let me emphasize for best results, don't let the wings sit in the corn flour/corn meal mixture. Fry the wings as soon as they are well coated with this final coating. Now, place several of the wings in the seasoned all-purpose flour, then in the egg wash, then in the corn flour/corn meal mixture, making sure that the wings are evenly coated. Immediately and very carefully drop the coated wings into the hot oil and fry, turning frequently, until golden and cooked through, about 7 to 8 minutes. Drain on paper towels and repeat the process, working in small batches, until all the wings are fried. Serve with the dipping sauce.

SOUP
SAFARI

Onion Roux Soup

If you're familiar with south Louisiana cooking, you've heard the term "roux" before. It's a basic first step in many recipes, the result of slowly browning a combination of equal parts of some kind of fat, such as oil, lard or butter, and flour. In this case, we get the delicious flavor of a roux by browning just the flour in a hot skillet. It's easy to do, but watch it carefully, for the flour browns very quickly once the skillet gets really hot! This soup tastes really spicy at first, but seems to become milder with each succeeding bite.

SEASONING MIX

1½ teaspoons salt
1 teaspoon ground cumin
1 teaspoon onion powder
¾ teaspoon cayenne
¾ teaspoon dried chervil leaves
¾ teaspoon dry mustard
¾ teaspoon paprika
½ teaspoon garlic powder

½ teaspoon black pepper
½ teaspoon ground dried New
    Mexico chile peppers (see pages 1
    and 2)
¼ teaspoon white pepper
¼ teaspoon ground savory
¼ teaspoon dried thyme leaves

¾ cup all-purpose flour
2 tablespoons unsalted butter
6½ cups onions, cut into ½-inch
    slices, each slice cut in half,
    about 3 medium-size onions
    (about 10 ounces each), in all

4 cups rich chicken stock or beef
    stock (see pages 5 and 6), in all
3 bay leaves
1 cup heavy cream

Combine the seasoning mix ingredients in a small bowl and mix well.

Preheat an 8-inch skillet over high heat for 2 minutes then add the flour. Whisking constantly to break up all the lumps, brown the flour by stirring and shaking the skillet until the flour is a light tan, then reduce the heat to medium and continue, whisking constantly, until the flour is a medium tan—about the color of coffee with a LOT of milk in it. The browning process will take about 8 minutes in all, but that's just a guide—look at the flour, not the timer. To keep the flour from burning, watch carefully and don't miss any spots when whisking, especially on the side of the skillet closest to you (which is harder to see), and be prepared to reduce the heat even more if necessary. Sift and set the browned flour aside. The last time we tested this recipe, we sifted out 1 tablespoon plus 1½ teaspoons of lumps from the flour, so you can see how important this step is. You can sift the flour first, but you'll still get some lumps as you brown it and will have to sift again afterwards.

Preheat a 4-quart pot over high heat for 4 minutes, then add the butter and half of the onions. Cover and cook, stirring and scraping the brown crust on the bottom of the pot every 2 minutes, until the onions begin to brown but the liquid in the onions is only beginning to evaporate, about 8 to 10 minutes. *We begin cooking the onions with the pot covered, because we want to be sure the heat gets to the center of the onions. They can't brown, though, with all their moisture, so later we remove the cover so the moisture can evaporate and they can begin to brown.* Uncover and continue to cook until the onions are caramelized, that is, browned and sweet-smelling, about 10 to 12 minutes longer. *This is another of those times when it's vital for you to watch what's happening in the pot rather than looking at the clock—the color and fragrance of the onions are a whole lot more important than the time of day!* Add the seasoning mix and the bay leaves, and stir and scrape the bottom of the pot for 30 seconds, then add ½ cup of the stock and cook, stirring constantly to break up any clumps of seasoning mix, for 1 minute. Stir in ½ cup of the stock and the browned flour. Stir and scrape until the flour is completely absorbed and the mixture forms a thick paste, adding a little more stock if necessary to make a paste. Whisk until all the lumps are completely broken up and scrape up the bottom of the pot, then whisk in the remaining stock and the remaining onions. Bring to a boil. During the time the soup is heating to the boiling point, stir every 2 or 3 minutes and check the bottom of the pot to be sure the flour is not sticking. This is an important step, because flour will settle until the liquid comes to a boil. As soon as the soup comes to a boil, reduce the heat to medium, re-cover, and simmer briskly, uncovering to stir every 5 minutes, until the mixture is reduced to the consistency of a rich gravy, about 15 minutes. Stir in the cream, bring just to a boil, and remove from the heat. Serve piping hot.

Fire-Roasted Pearl Onion Soup

Photograph No. 3

MAKES ABOUT 5 CUPS

Because they're so small, the pearl onions may be a little tricky to roast—but you can get the job done with a little ingenuity. If you have a grilling rack with small holes, you can use that over the open flame, or just roast them in a 500° oven. If your onions are larger than ½ inch, after roasting squeeze them gently and pop off one or more layers until they are the right size. Also, snip off any charred black stems that might remain after roasting.

SEASONING MIX

2 teaspoons salt
1 teaspoon ground coriander
1 teaspoon onion powder
1 teaspoon paprika
1 teaspoon ground dried New Mexico
   chile peppers (see pages 1 and 2)
¾ teaspoon cayenne
¾ teaspoon ground ginger

½ teaspoon ground cumin
½ teaspoon ground cardamom
½ teaspoon ground cinnamon
½ teaspoon garlic powder
½ teaspoon ground nutmeg
½ teaspoon ground dried chipotle
   chile peppers (see pages 1 and 2)
¼ teaspoon white pepper

8 tablespoons (1 stick) unsalted
   butter
¼ cup all-purpose flour
2 cups vegetable stock (see pages 5
   and 6), in all

2 cups heavy cream
40 pearl onions, fire-roasted (see
   page 4)

Combine the seasoning mix ingredients in a small bowl and mix well.

In a heavy 4-quart pot over high heat melt the butter. Watch closely, and as soon as the butter is melted add 1 tablespoon plus 2 teaspoons of the seasoning mix and whisk it in well. Add the flour and whisk constantly just until the mixture darkens a little but is not yet brown, about 2 minutes. Stir in 1 cup of the stock and, whisking constantly to keep the flour from settling, bring the mixture to a full boil—the liquid is likely to boil very fast, perhaps in just a few seconds, because the pot is very hot and you're not adding very much liquid at this point. Quickly add the cream, whisking it in well, and cook just until the mixture returns to a boil. Immediately add the remaining cup of stock, the remaining seasoning mix, and the roasted pearl onions. When the mixture returns again to a boil, reduce the heat to medium and simmer briskly, whisking every 2 to 3 minutes, for 10 minutes. Remove from the heat and serve at once.

Shrimp and Cream Cheese Soup

MAKES 4 MAIN-COURSE OR 8 APPETIZER SERVINGS

This soup is a big favorite with everyone who's tasted it so far! Who am I to argue? I love it too! You can use low-fat or nonfat cream cheese if you wish.

SEASONING MIX

1¼ teaspoons paprika
1¼ teaspoons salt
1 teaspoon dried oregano leaves
¾ teaspoon dried chervil leaves
¾ teaspoon ground ginger
¾ teaspoon onion powder

¾ teaspoon dried thyme leaves
½ teaspoon garlic powder
¼ teaspoon cayenne
¼ teaspoon black pepper
¼ teaspoon white pepper

4 cups shrimp stock (see pages 5 and 6), in all
4 ounces cream cheese, softened
½ cup all-purpose flour
2 tablespoons olive oil
2 cups chopped onions, about 2 small
¾ cup chopped bell peppers, about 1 small

1 cup chopped celery, about 2 stalks
2 teaspoons minced fresh garlic, about 2 cloves
½ cup thinly sliced green onions, about 6 stalks
2 cups sliced mushrooms
1 pound peeled shrimp

Combine the seasoning mix ingredients in a small bowl and mix well.

Combine ½ cup stock and the cream cheese in a blender and process until thoroughly blended.

In a heavy 8-inch skillet over high heat, brown the flour, stirring constantly to prevent burning, until the flour is a tan color. Remove the flour from the skillet to stop the browning, sift, and set it aside.

In a heavy 4-quart pot over high heat, heat the oil just until it begins to smoke, about 3 to 4 minutes. Add the onions, bell peppers, celery, garlic, green onions, and 1 tablespoon seasoning mix. Cook, stirring and scraping the bottom of the pot every 4 or 5 minutes, until the vegetables are well browned, about 20 to 25 minutes. Add ½ cup stock and the remaining seasoning mix. Stir in the browned flour until it is completely absorbed— the mixture will be thick and pasty. Add the remaining stock, mushrooms, and green onions, and stir thoroughly. Bring to a full boil, then stir in the cream cheese/stock mixture. Return to a full boil, then add the shrimp and return just to a boil. Reduce the heat to low and simmer just until the shrimp are pink and opaque, about 3 minutes. Remove from the heat and serve hot.

Cream of Broccoli Soup

MAKES 8 APPETIZER SERVINGS OR 4 MAIN-COURSE SERVINGS

This flavorful, creamy soup is just the thing on a cold day! If you're watching your intake of dietary fat, simply substitute 2 cups of nonfat sour cream for the heavy cream and regular sour cream we call for. And if finding yucca is difficult where you shop, you can use 4 cups of peeled, diced potatoes plus 1 tablespoon sugar. The result will be a little different, but it will still be delicious.

SEASONING MIX

2 teaspoons salt
1 teaspoon dried basil leaves
1 teaspoon dry mustard
1 teaspoon onion powder
1 teaspoon tarragon leaves
¾ teaspoon cayenne
¾ teaspoon garlic powder

¾ teaspoon ground ginger
¾ teaspoon white pepper
¾ teaspoon dried thyme leaves
½ teaspoon ground cinnamon
½ teaspoon ground nutmeg
¼ teaspoon black pepper

2 tablespoons vegetable oil
2 cups chopped onions, about 2
  small, in all
2 cups chopped celery, about 4
  stalks, in all
7 cups chicken stock (see pages 5
  and 6), in all
4 cups yucca (see page 172), 1
  whole yucca, about 2 pounds,

peeled, quartered lengthwise
  (the tough central stalk
  discarded), then diced
2 to 2½ cups broccoli stems, peeled
  and diced
4 cups broccoli florets
1 cup heavy cream
1 cup sour cream (see page 3)

Combine the seasoning mix ingredients in a small bowl and mix well.

In a 4-quart pot over high heat, heat the oil just until it begins to smoke, about 3 to 4 minutes. Add 1 cup of the onions, 1 cup of the celery, and 2 tablespoons of the seasoning mix. Cook, stirring and scraping the pot every 1 or 2 minutes, until the vegetables are very lightly browned, about 7 minutes. Add 2 cups of stock, then stir and scrape the pan bottom well. When the mixture returns to a boil, add the yucca, the remaining onions, the remaining celery, the broccoli stems, and the remaining seasoning mix. From this point on, the soup is to be cooked covered; uncover the pot only when you need to stir or add an ingredient. Cook, stirring every 3 or 4 minutes, for 12 minutes, then stir in 1 cup of stock. Continue to cook, stirring every 4 or 5 minutes, for 15 minutes. Add 1 more cup of stock and cook, stirring every 3 or 4 minutes, for 12 more minutes. Whisk the soup thoroughly to release the starch from the yucca, then add 3 cups of the stock. Add the broccoli florets and cook, stirring and scraping the bottom of the pot every 1 or 2 minutes, for 7 minutes. Stir in the heavy cream and the sour cream just until they are entirely blended in, then remove the soup from the heat and serve immediately.

Crab Bisque

Photograph No. 3

MAKES 10 APPETIZER SERVINGS OR 5 MAIN-COURSE SERVINGS

Many of my recipes call for browning the vegetables, but this recipe is quite different because the vegetables are "sweated" instead, or cooked in their own juices over high heat just to the moment before they would brown. Allowing the vegetable mixture to brown would overpower the delicate flavor of the crab meat. I think the combination of the sweet potatoes' pretty color and the cream looks terrific! And it tastes great!.

SEASONING MIX

2 teaspoons dried basil leaves
2 teaspoons salt
2 teaspoons onion powder
2 teaspoons chopped lemon zest (see page 7) or grated lemon peel
2 teaspoons chopped orange zest (see page 7) or grated orange peel
1½ teaspoons dry mustard
1 teaspoon garlic powder

½ teaspoon cayenne
½ teaspoon ground cinnamon
½ teaspoon ground nutmeg
½ teaspoon white pepper
½ teaspoon ground dried ancho chile peppers (see pages 1 and 2)
½ teaspoon ground dried chipotle chile peppers (see pages 1 and 2)
¼ teaspoon black pepper

2 tablespoons vegetable oil
3 cups chopped onions, about 3 small, in all
3 cups chopped bell peppers, about 3 medium, in all
2 cups chopped celery, about 4 stalks
1½ cups fresh fennel bulb (see page 167), about 1 medium-size bulb, trimmed and diced into ¼-inch pieces

4 cups sweet potatoes, peeled and diced into ¼-inch pieces, about 2 medium-size potatoes
7 cups crab stock (preferred), or seafood stock, or shrimp stock (see pages 5 and 6), in all
1 tablespoon minced fresh garlic, about 3 cloves
4 tablespoons unsalted butter
1 cup heavy cream
½ cup chopped fresh sweet basil
1 pound lump crab meat, picked over for shells and cartilage

Combine the seasoning mix ingredients in a small bowl and mix well.

In a heavy 4-quart pot over high heat, heat the oil just until it begins to smoke, about 3 to 4 minutes. Add 2 cups of the onions, 2 cups of the bell peppers, the celery, fennel, sweet potatoes and 1 tablespoon of the seasoning mix. Stir well, cover and cook, uncovering to stir every 2 minutes, until the mixture begins to stick hard, but before it begins to brown, about 8 minutes. *Reduce the heat if necessary to prevent scorching, but keep cooking and scraping, because this process develops the flavors of the vegetables.* Add 2 cups of the stock, scrape the bottom and sides of the pot well, then add the garlic, butter, the remaining onions, the remaining bell peppers, and the remaining seasoning mix. Continue to cook over medium-high heat, stirring and scraping every 3 minutes, and scraping almost constantly during the last 5 minutes to prevent the mixture from browning, for a total of 15 minutes. Add the remaining stock and scrape the bottom and sides of the pot. Whisk the mixture vigorously, breaking up the sweet potatoes, for 2 or 3 minutes. Stir in the cream and basil, bring just to a boil, reduce the heat to low, then cover and simmer for 20 minutes. Stir in the crab meat, return just to a simmer, and remove the bisque from the heat. Serve piping hot.

Uncle Sy's Chicken Soup

Photograph No. 3

MAKES 8 APPETIZER SERVINGS OR 4 MAIN-COURSE SERVINGS

You don't have to be sick to want some of this soup! Besides the usual carrots, onions, and celery, it has wonderful yellow squash and fresh tomatoes, so you're getting more vitamins than even in old-fashioned chicken soup, and our carefully balanced seasonings will send your taste buds flying high.

This soup is named for "Uncle" Sy Stemp, an old friend and business advisor, whose gentle humor is as comforting as a good bowl of soup.

SEASONING MIX

2½ teaspoons salt	¾ teaspoon garlic powder
1½ teaspoons dry mustard	¾ teaspoon onion powder
1¼ teaspoons dried chervil leaves	¾ teaspoon black pepper
1¼ teaspoons dried marjoram leaves	½ teaspoon cayenne
¾ teaspoon dill weed	½ teaspoon white pepper

1 (3- to 3½- pound) chicken, cut into 8 pieces
2 tablespoons corn starch
8 cups chicken stock (see pages 5 and 6), in all
2 tablespoons vegetable oil
3 cups chopped onions, about 2 medium
1½ cups chopped celery, about 3 stalks
1 cup yellow squash, diced into ½-inch pieces
1 cup zucchini, diced into ½-inch pieces
1½ cups carrots, diced into ½-inch pieces
1½ teaspoons minced fresh garlic, about 2 small cloves
2 cups chopped peeled fresh tomatoes (see page 7)

Combine the seasoning mix ingredients in a small bowl and mix well.

Sprinkle the chicken evenly with 2 tablespoons of the seasoning mix and rub it in well.

Dissolve the corn starch in 2 tablespoons of cool stock and set it aside.

In a heavy 4-quart pot over high heat, heat the oil just until it begins to smoke, about 3 to 4 minutes. Add the chicken in batches, large pieces first and skin sides down first, and cook, turning every 2 minutes, until golden brown, about 8 minutes per batch. Remove the chicken from the pot and set it aside.

To the same pot add the onions and celery. Cook, stirring and scraping the brown bits every 2 or 3 minutes, until the vegetables are browned, about 5 to 7 minutes. Add 3 cups of stock and bring to a full boil, stirring and scraping every 4 or 5 minutes. Add the remaining seasoning mix and continue to boil until most of the liquid evaporates, about 12 minutes. Add the remaining stock and bring to a boil. Stir in the corn starch/stock mixture and, whisking frequently, return to a boil. Add the yellow squash, zucchini, carrots, garlic, and tomatoes to the pot, stir well, return the chicken and the accumulated juices to the pot, then bring to a rolling boil. Reduce the heat to low and simmer just until the chicken is cooked through, about 12 to 18 minutes. Serve with rice or pasta.

Cauliflower Duck Soup

MAKES 8 APPETIZER SERVINGS OR 4-MAIN COURSE SERVINGS

Take a short cut: ask your butcher to skin and cut up your duck for you. Ducks are much harder to skin than chickens! If you can't get someone else to skin the duck, try placing it in the freezer, and as soon as the surface is hard, skin it. Cauliflower is a strong-flavored vegetable, but the duck can hold its own, and the addition of the crisp skin (cracklings) and green onions on top gives this soup a special flavor and crunch that set it apart.

SEASONING MIX

1½ teaspoons salt	½ teaspoon ground ginger
1 teaspoon paprika	½ teaspoon dry mustard
¾ teaspoon onion powder	½ teaspoon black pepper
½ teaspoon ground coriander	½ teaspoon ground savory
½ teaspoon ground cumin	¼ teaspoon cayenne
½ teaspoon garlic powder	¼ teaspoon white pepper

1 (4½- to 5-pound) duck, cut into 8 pieces	1 cup chopped celery, about 2 stalks
4¼ cups duck stock, preferred, or chicken stock (see pages 5 and 6), in all	3 cups small cauliflower florets
	½ cup heavy cream
6 tablespoons all-purpose flour	¼ cup thinly sliced green onions, about 3 stalks
1 cup chopped onions, about 1 small (5 ounces)	2 cups cooked white rice

Combine the seasoning mix ingredients in a small bowl and mix well.

Remove the skin and excess fat from the duck pieces, dice the skin and fat into small pieces and set them aside. Sprinkle the skinless duck pieces evenly with 2 tablespoons plus 1 teaspoon of seasoning mix and rub it in well.

Place the diced skin and fat into a heavy 4-quart pot over low heat and cook slowly, stirring every 1 or 2 minutes, until the skin has rendered as much fat as possible and is very crisp. *The time to render the fat will vary widely, depending upon how much fat there is. Be careful not to let the skin burn, as it browns very quickly—you want to render all the fat but not burn it. If you see blue smoke, lower the heat immediately.* When the fat is rendered and the skin is just crisp and brown, turn off the heat and carefully pour the rendered fat and crisp skin (cracklings) into a strainer over a bowl. Set the drained cracklings aside on paper towels, and reserve the duck fat.

To the now empty pot add ½ cup stock and stir and scrape the bottom thoroughly to loosen all the browned bits. Pour this stock, with the brown bits (they add great flavor) back into the container that holds the rest of the stock. Wash the pot and dry it, then pour the reserved duck fat back into the clean pot and place it over high heat. When the fat is hot, brown the duck in batches, turning once a minute, for 7 to 8 minutes per batch. Remove the duck from the pot and set it aside. To the same pot add ¾ cup stock, the flour, and the remaining seasoning mix. If the flour forms lumps, use a whisk to break them up. Cook, almost constantly stirring and scraping the bottom of the pot, until the mixture is lightly browned and sticks hard, about 3 to 4 minutes. Add 1 cup of stock, scrape the bottom of the pot to loosen the brown bits, and add a little more stock if necessary. Add the onions, celery, and 1½ cups of stock. Return the duck and the accumulated juices to the pot together with any remaining stock. Bring just to a boil, reduce the heat to low and simmer until the duck is tender, about 15 minutes. Add the cauliflower and submerge it completely into the liquid. Cook, scraping the pot bottom once or twice until the cauliflower is tender, about 6 to 8 minutes. Stir in the cream, then bring just to a boil and remove from the heat.

For each main course portion, serve 1½ cups of soup with ½ cup rice and 2 pieces of duck, and for an appetizer portion, serve ¾ cup of soup with ¼ cup of rice and 1 piece of duck. If you prefer, you can serve the duck on a plate alongside the soup in its bowl. Or, if you like a hearty soup that's easy to eat, once the duck is done and cool enough to handle, cut the meat off the bones and return it to the soup. Garnish with the green onions and cracklings.

Shrimp and Greens Gumbo

MAKES 4 MAIN-COURSE OR 8 APPETIZER SERVINGS

In south Louisiana many good cooks make gumbo mostly with greens and seasonings, and maybe not a lot else. This version, with a dark and rich-tasting roux, has lots of greens, plus we've added andouille, tasso, and shrimp for a distinctive and satisfying flavor. We've also fired up the soup with four kinds of peppers, so watch out, Mama, here she comes!

SEASONING MIX

1½ teaspoons salt
1 teaspoon dried basil leaves
1 teaspoon paprika
¾ teaspoon onion powder
¾ teaspoon dried thyme leaves
½ teaspoon cayenne
½ teaspoon garlic powder

½ teaspoon ground ginger
½ teaspoon dry mustard
½ teaspoon dried oregano leaves
½ teaspoon black pepper
½ teaspoon ground dried ancho chili
    peppers (see pages 1 and 2)
¼ teaspoon white pepper

½ cup all-purpose flour
2 tablespoons vegetable oil
1 cup chopped celery
½ cup chopped green bell peppers
½ cup chopped red bell peppers
½ cup chopped yellow bell peppers
2 cups chopped onions, about 1
    large
¼ pound andouille (see page 165)
    or your favorite smoked pork
    sausage, quartered lengthwise,
    and cut into ½-inch pieces
¼ pound tasso (see page 172) or
    smoked ham, diced into ¼-inch
    pieces

2 tablespoons unsalted butter
6 cups shrimp stock (see page 6)
8 cups mixed greens, such as
    collard, mustard, or turnip
    greens, washed, stemmed, and
    chopped
1½ teaspoons minced fresh garlic,
    about 2 small cloves
½ pound peeled shrimp, either
    21-25 count or 26-30 count (see
    page 4)
½ cup thinly sliced green onions,
    about 6 stalks
2 tablespoons minced fresh parsley

Combine the seasoning mix ingredients in a small bowl and mix well.

In a heavy skillet over high heat, brown the flour, stirring and shaking the skillet to prevent burning, until the flour is the color of milk chocolate. Immediately remove the flour from the skillet to stop the browning, sift and set it aside.

In a heavy 4-quart pot over high heat, heat the oil just until it begins to smoke, about 3 to 4 minutes. Add the celery, bell peppers, half of the onions, the andouille, tasso, and 1 tablespoon plus 1 teaspoon of the seasoning mix. *Caution: During the next long cooking period, a total of 25 minutes, you must take care to avoid scorching the ingredients on the bottom of the pot. Watch closely even when you're not stirring, and if necessary lower the heat or add a little stock even before the recipe tells you to. You're going to have plenty of stock to add later, so use some of it now if you need to. It's more important to use your good judgment and end up with something wonderful to eat than to follow directions slavishly.* Cook, stirring every 4 or 5 minutes, for 15 minutes, then add the remaining onions and the remaining seasoning mix. Continue to cook, stirring and scraping the bottom of the pot every 2 or 3 minutes, for 10 minutes. Add the butter, and as it melts scrape the pot bottom thoroughly to prevent sticking. Add the browned flour and stir until it is completely absorbed. Add 1 cup stock and stir well for a minute or so, then add the greens. Cook, turning the greens over (you'll notice that they wilt and reduce in volume as they cook), stirring and scraping the pot bottom every 2 or 3 minutes to prevent sticking, for 10 minutes. Add the garlic and the remaining stock and bring to a boil. Continue to cook over high heat for 10 minutes, then reduce the heat to medium and simmer briskly for 20 minutes. Add the shrimp and, as soon as they are pink and opaque add the green onions and parsley. Remove from the heat, stir gently, and serve with hot white rice.

LAGNIAPPE

A LITTLE SOMETHING FROM ALL OVER

Lagniappe is a New Orleans word that means "a little something extra," such as the cookie given to a child by the baker when the mother buys dinner rolls. In this chapter you'll find little extras like unusual salads, a pair of relishes, and information on my original blackening method.

Orzo Salad

MAKES 12 SIDE-DISH SERVINGS OR 6 MAIN-COURSE SERVINGS

Here's a great salad that's totally vegetarian, yet has lots of protein from the beans. The tangy dressing, with its vinegars and pepper sauce, is the perfect complement to the sweetness of the bell peppers and brown sugar. Notice that both varieties of beans are to be soaked overnight, so plan ahead. If you forget, don't panic, just boil them vigorously for five minutes, then let them sit in the liquid for 1 hour, drain, and carry on with the recipe.

SALAD

2 cups uncooked orzo pasta
1 cup dried Appaloosa beans (see page 165) or butterscotch beans (see page 165), soaked overnight and drained

1 cup dried black beans, soaked overnight and drained
2 cups fresh baby green beans, trimmed and cut into 1-inch lengths

VINAIGRETTE

SEASONING MIX

1½ teaspoons dried dill weed
1½ teaspoons onion powder
1½ teaspoons ground dried New Mexico chile peppers (see pages 1 and 2)
1 teaspoon paprika

1 teaspoon ground dried ancho chile peppers (see pages 1 and 2)
1 teaspoon ground dried árbol chile peppers (see pages 1 and 2)
1 teaspoon salt
½ teaspoon ground cumin

½ cup minced green bell peppers, about ½ medium
½ cup minced red bell peppers, about ½ medium
½ cup minced yellow bell peppers, about ½ medium
¼ cup minced shallots
2 tablespoons light brown sugar

¼ cup vegetable oil
¼ cup cane vinegar (see page 172)
¼ cup balsamic vinegar
2 tablespoons fresh lime juice
2 tablespoons Chef Paul Prudhomme's Magic Pepper Sauce®
2 tablespoons sesame oil

In a 6-quart pot over high heat, bring 2 quarts of water to a boil. Add the orzo, return to a boil, and boil until the pasta is cooked, about 10 to 12 minutes. Remove the pasta from the pot and rinse in a colander under hot water for 1 minute, then under cold water until the pasta is cool. Drain thoroughly and set aside.

In a 6-quart pot over high heat, bring 3 quarts of water to a boil. Add the Appaloosa (or butterscotch) beans, return to a boil, then reduce the heat to medium and simmer briskly until the beans are tender but not mushy, about 1 hour. Drain the Appaloosa (or butterscotch) beans and set them aside to cool.

In a 6-quart pot over high heat, bring 3 quarts of water to a boil. Add the black beans, return to a boil, then reduce the heat to medium and simmer until the beans are tender but not mushy, about 1 hour. Drain the black beans and set them aside to cool.

Combine the seasoning mix ingredients in a small bowl and mix well.

Combine the vinaigrette ingredients in a medium-size bowl, add 1 tablespoon plus 1 teaspoon of the seasoning mix, and whisk until well combined. Set aside.

When all the ingredients are at room temperature, combine them in a large bowl and mix in the remaining seasoning mix. Whisk the vinaigrette dressing to combine again and pour it over the salad. Toss gently to coat all parts of the salad with the dressing and refrigerate until cold. Serve 2 cups per person for a main course, or 1 cup for a side-dish serving.

Salmon Salad on Cassava Crispies

Photograph No. 4

MAKES 4 SERVINGS

This layered delight provides contrasts of flavors, textures, and even temperatures! A portion of tangy dressing forms the base for everything else. Next up is a crisp, hot, and delicious patty made primarily of cassava (yucca), and that's topped with lightly pan-fried fresh salmon, pink and tempting and perfectly seasoned. The salmon is crowned with cool julienne strips of three complementary vegetables—sweet potatoes, bok choy, and jicama—and the final touch is a sprinkling of chopped fresh cilantro leaves. This salad, whose recipe was developed by Chef Crispin Pasia, is beautiful, so serve it as the highlight of a festive lunch or supper. Don't waste the bok choy leaves—they're great in a stir-fry!

SEASONING MIX

1 tablespoon plus 1 teaspoon salt	1 tablespoon onion powder
1 tablespoon ground cumin	2 teaspoons dried basil leaves
1 tablespoon ground dried Anaheim chile peppers (see pages 1 and 2)	2 teaspoons garlic powder
	2 teaspoons dry mustard

2 teaspoons ground dried ancho chile peppers (see pages 1 and 2)

1 teaspoon black pepper

1½ teaspoons ground ginger

½ teaspoon white pepper

SALMON

2 (8-ounce) salmon fillets

2 teaspoons vegetable oil

SESAME MIXTURE

4 tablespoons (½ stick) unsalted butter

1 cup chopped onions, about 1 small (5 ounces)

¼ cup olive oil

½ cup sesame seeds

1 cup chopped celery, about 2 stalks

CASSAVA CRISPIES

1 yucca (cassava, see page 172), about 12 inches long and 3 inches in diameter, peeled

DRESSING

1 cup sweet potatoes, diced into ½-inch cubes, about 1 very small, 11 ounces

1 cup yogurt (see page 3)

MARINATED VEGETABLES

1 cup sweet potatoes, cut into julienne strips (see page 3)

1 cup jicama (see page 167), cut into julienne strips (see page 3)

1 cup bok choy, white parts only, cut into julienne strips (see page 3)

Juice of 1 orange, about ¼ cup

Juice of 2 limes, about ¼ cup

¼ cup cane vinegar (see page 172)

ASSEMBLY

2 tablespoons plus 2 teaspoons vegetable oil, in all

8 tablespoons loosely packed chopped cilantro, in all

Combine the seasoning mix ingredients in a small bowl and mix well.

Sprinkle each side of each salmon fillet evenly with 1 teaspoon of the seasoning mix, then gently rub it in.

SALMON In a 12-inch skillet over high heat, heat the vegetable oil just until it begins to smoke, about 3 to 4 minutes. Place the salmon fillets in the skillet and cook, turning once, until they are dark golden brown on the surface, but still very tender and soft inside, about 3 to 4 minutes per side. Set the fillets aside until they are cool enough to handle, then with a fork shred the fish into large flakes. Refrigerate until ready to use.

SESAME MIXTURE In a 12-inch skillet over high heat, melt the butter with the olive oil. When the butter begins to sizzle, add the sesame seeds, onions, celery, and 2 tablespoons of the seasoning mix. Cook, stirring once a minute, until the mixture begins to darken, about 5 to 7 minutes. Remove from the heat, spread the mixture on a sheet pan, and set aside to cool.

CASSAVA CRISPIES Coarsely shred the yucca on a grater.

In a large mixing bowl, toss the grated yucca with a generous ½ cup of the sesame mixture and 1 tablespoon of the seasoning mix, making sure that the ingredients are evenly distributed and the yucca pieces are well separated and not sticking to each other. Set aside.

DRESSING In a 1-quart saucepan over high heat, bring 2 cups of water to a boil. Add the diced sweet potatoes, return to a brisk simmer, and cook just until the potatoes are cooked through and soft, about 20 minutes. Drain and set aside to cool.

In a blender combine the diced sweet potatoes, the remaining 1 cup of the sesame mixture, the yogurt, and the remaining seasoning mix. Process at medium speed until smooth and set aside.

MARINATED VEGETABLES In a 1-quart saucepan over high heat, bring 2 cups of water to a boil. Add the julienne strips of sweet potatoes and simmer just until the potatoes are soft but not mushy, about 2 minutes (these sweet potatoes will cook much faster than the diced ones because they are cut so much smaller). Drain well and cool, and place in a small bowl or 1-quart plastic zipper bag, along with the bok choy and jicama. Add the orange juice, lime juice, and vinegar, and marinate, turning the mixture every 7 or 8 minutes (this is really easy if you use a tightly closed zipper bag), for 30 minutes. Then drain and discard the liquid.

ASSEMBLY In a 10-inch skillet over high heat, heat 2 teaspoons vegetable oil just until it begins to smoke, about 3 to 4 minutes. Add ¾ cup of the yucca mixture and flatten it out until is resembles crispy hash browns. Cook, turning every 45 seconds, for 3 minutes, then remove from the skillet and drain on paper towels. Repeat the process to make the other three yucca crispies.

For each serving, place ½ cup of the sauce on a plate. Place 1 of the crispies on top of the sauce. Mound 4 ounces of salmon on top of the crispy, and arrange ¾ cup of the julienne vegetables over the salmon. Top with 2 tablespoons of the chopped cilantro.

Crawfish and Brown Rice Salad

MAKES 4 SERVINGS

I really like it when I can come up with new and different taste combinations, so you know I enjoyed creating this recipe! It's got several contrasts—in flavor, texture and color—which give it a depth that you don't usually find in salads. Notice that you can make this with shrimp, clams, or fish—use what you like that looks fresh at the market. When we taped the television program, we used barley instead of rice, because I think barley is great and under-used in this country. Try rice one time and barley the next and see which one you like better.

SEASONING MIX

2 teaspoons salt
2 teaspoons dried basil leaves
1½ teaspoons onion powder
1 teaspoon cayenne
1 teaspoon Chinese 5-spice powder
   (see page 166)

1 teaspoon ground coriander
1 teaspoon ground dried pasilla chile
   peppers (see pages 1 and 2)
½ teaspoon garlic powder

1 cup uncooked short-grain brown
   rice
3 cups crawfish stock, or seafood
   stock, or chicken stock (see
   pages 5 and 6), in all
½ teaspoon salt
1 cup chopped onions, about 1
   small (5 ounces)
1 cup chopped red bell peppers,
   about 1 medium
1 tablespoon olive oil
1 tablespoon minced fresh garlic,
   about 3 cloves
1 tablespoon white wine vinegar

2 tablespoons cane vinegar (see
   page 172)
1 tablespoon fresh lime juice
½ cup pumpkin seeds, toasted (see
   page 7)
1 tablespoon plus 1 teaspoon
   lightly packed dark brown sugar
1 pound crawfish tails or small
   peeled boiled shrimp (26-30
   count, see page 4), or small
   steamed clams, or flaked cooked
   fish
½ cup chopped green onions, green
   parts only, about 6 stalks

To remove the excess starch from the rice (which would cause it to be too sticky after cooking), wash it before cooking. Place the rice in a large bowl in the sink under gently running water—don't let the water run too fast, or it might wash the rice itself out of the bowl, instead of just the excess starch. Cup your hands and scoop up a handful of rice. Hold your hands so that the rice is directly under the running water, and rub your hands back and forth and up and down,

42

so that the water rinses away the starch as you scrub the rice. After about 30 seconds, release that rice back into the bowl and scoop up another handful of rice. Continue scrubbing handfuls of rice until the rinse water runs clear, then transfer the rinsed rice to a colander to let the excess water drain away.

Combine the seasoning mix ingredients in a small bowl and mix well.

In a 2-quart pot over high heat bring 2½ cups of the stock and the salt to a boil and add the rice. Cover, reduce the heat to low and cook, without stirring, until the rice is tender and the water is absorbed, about 45 minutes. Remove from the heat and set aside to cool.

Preheat a large skillet over high heat for 3 minutes, then add the onions and bell peppers. Cook, stirring once a minute, for 4 minutes, then stir in the olive oil. Cook and stir for 2 minutes and stir in the garlic. Cook and stir for 2 minutes longer, and stir in 2 tablespoons of the seasoning mix. Cook and stir for 2 minutes, then remove from the heat, transfer to a platter, and refrigerate while you make the dressing.

In a blender combine the remaining ½ cup stock, the two vinegars, lime juice, and toasted seeds and process for 30 seconds. Add ¼ cup of the cooked rice, the remaining seasoning mix, and the brown sugar. Process until smooth, about 1½ minutes longer, and set aside.

Make the salad by gently combining ¾ cup of the cooked rice with the cooled vegetable mixture and the crawfish (or shrimp, clams, or fish).

For each serving, place ¼ cup of the rice (I like to mold it in a small cup and turn it out neatly) in the center of a large salad plate or luncheon-size plate. Surround the rice with 1 cup of the salad, then carefully ladle about 3 ounces (3/8 cup) of the sauce around the edge of the salad. Garnish with 2 tablespoons of the green onions. Repeat the steps to make the remaining salads and serve at once. It looks terrific the way it is, but when you eat it you'll want to mix it all up together so you'll get some of each flavor and texture in every bite.

Pico de Gallo

This sauce, whose name means "Rooster's Beak," adds a peppery sharpness to dishes from South of the Border, including several in this book, and is perfect as a dip with corn chips. My thanks go to Sean O'Meara, who developed this version of a popular sauce. Serve slightly chilled or at room temperature. Olé!

1 tablespoon white vinegar
1 tablespoon plus 1 teaspoon Chef
  Paul Prudhomme's Magic
  Pepper Sauce®
¼ teaspoon ground dried árbol
  chile peppers (see pages 1 and 2)
1 teaspoon light brown sugar
¼ teaspoon ground cumin
3 medium-size tomatoes, peeled
  (see page 7) and chopped, about
  2 cups
¾ cup onions, diced into ¼-inch
  pieces
¼ cup bell pepper, diced into
  ¼-inch pieces

¼ cup celery, diced into ¼-inch
  pieces
½ teaspoon minced fresh garlic,
  about ½ clove
1 tablespoon minced fresh ginger
2 tablespoons minced fresh poblano
  chile peppers (see pages 1 and 2)
2 tablespoons minced fresh serrano
  chile peppers (see pages 1 and 2)
2 tablespoons minced fresh
  Anaheim chile peppers (see pages
  1 and 2)
1 minced fresh bird's eye or Thai
  chile pepper (see pages 1 and 2),
  optional; use it if you like your
  Pico de Gallo very hot

Combine the vinegar and Magic Pepper Sauce in a large bowl. Stir in the árbol chiles, brown sugar and cumin until the sugar is dissolved. Add the remaining ingredients and stir until well blended. Cover and refrigerate for at least 4 hours, preferably overnight, before serving.

Papaya Dipping Sauce

This recipe makes a great salad dressing, especially for fresh fruit salads, as well as a perfect dipping sauce for fried shrimp, battered and fried vegetables, tempura, our Deep-Fried Sweet Potato Chips (page 132) and just about anything else you can think of. It has just the right balance of sweet and tangy.

¼ cup chopped onion
1 (1-pound) ripe papaya, peeled and chopped, including the seeds, about 1¼ cups (see page 170)
2 tablespoons sugar
½ cup sweet rice wine vinegar

2 tablespoons white balsamic vinegar (see page 172)
1 tablespoon cane vinegar (see page 172)
1 cup cotton seed oil or vegetable oil
1 teaspoon salt
¼ teaspoon white pepper

Combine all the ingredients in a blender or food processor and process until well blended and smooth, with the consistency of a thin mayonnaise. Serve at room temperature, and refrigerate any leftover sauce.

Honey Mustard Corn Chow-Chow

Photograph No. 10

MAKES ABOUT 3 CUPS

While many regions of the country boast of their own particular corn relishes, it's not likely you'll come across any just like this one! The fresh chile peppers give it a sparkle all its own, and the dried chipotle peppers impart a great smoky flavor that really sets off the corn and our non-traditional vinegars. And I'll let you in on a secret: if you add a pound of oysters to this relish and let the mixture marinate for three or four hours, you'll make Pickled Oysters!

2 (11-ounce) cans whole kernel corn, Green Giant Niblet® brand preferred, drained, about 3 cups
3 tablespoons Creole mustard (see page 167)
2 tablespoons Chef Paul Prudhomme's Magic Pepper Sauce®
¼ cup cane vinegar (see page 172)
¼ cup white balsamic vinegar (see page 172)

¼ cup honey
1 cup fresh Anaheim chile peppers or banana peppers (see pages 1 and 2), diced into ¼-inch pieces
2 teaspoons minced fresh garlic, about 2 cloves
1 tablespoon minced fresh ginger
½ teaspoon ground dried chipotle chile peppers (see pages 1 and 2)
½ teaspoon salt

Combine all the ingredients in a large bowl and stir until well blended. Refrigerate for at least 4 hours, preferably overnight, before serving, and refrigerate any leftover relish.

Blackening and Bronzing

When I developed the blackening method of cooking—redfish at the beginning but later other kinds of fish, fowl and meat—I truly had no idea how popular (and imitated) it would become! It's really a simple technique, and one that produces exciting results.

Remember that these recipes should only be used with the very freshest products available. This cooking method accents the taste of whatever you're cooking. If it is a poor quality product or seafood that smells fishy, the cooking method accents these poor qualities. If it's a fresh, high quality product, especially fish or seafood without a strong smell, that will also be accented.

Blackening

For blackening, you need a cast iron skillet to stand up to the intense heat. And because the method produces a large amount of heat and smoke, unless you have a commercial kitchen range hood, you'll want to work outdoors on a gas grill or burner.

Here's the procedure for blackening:

Melt unsalted butter or margarine and set it aside. Heat a large cast iron skillet over very high heat until it is extremely hot, at least 500°. It will take about 10 minutes to reach that temperature.

The item to be blackened should be at room temperature (so the butter will adhere but not congeal). If you must use cold meat or fish, you will have to adjust the cooking time and turn the item almost continuously to avoid burning and to lock in the juices. Turning the item continuously forces the juices to remain in the center. For example, when you see the little drops of juice appear on the top of a grilling hamburger, they are being pushed up by the heat underneath.

Brush one side of the item evenly with the melted butter. Sprinkle (don't pour) the desired Magic Seasoning Blend on the buttered side of the fish (or bird or meat) and carefully place it, buttered and seasoned side down, in the hot, dry skillet. Brush the top with melted butter and sprinkle the top with Magic Seasoning Blend.

Cook, turning frequently, until done. The cooking time will vary according to what you are blackening, but 4 minutes total cooking time is usual.

That's it! Because the method is simple, any variation will make a dramatic difference. Be sure the skillet is hot enough, and absolutely dry. Be sure not to overseason—the herbs and spices should highlight the taste, rather than hide it. And you don't want to overcook the fillet, chop or steak—there's a big difference between blackened and burned. Avoid a burned, bitter taste by wiping out the skillet between batches.

After cooking the first batch, wipe out the skillet to remove all flaked brown or black pieces. After the second batch, the skillet should be burned out by inverting the skillet over an open flame for about 3 to 5 minutes, then wiping with a heavy cloth until the skillet looks clean and no large particles continue to appear on the cloth. Then, before continuing to cook, use a fresh cloth with a small amount of oil on it to wipe the skillet one more time. Use this same procedure—burning out, wiping until clean, then wiping with the lightly oiled clean cloth—when you are finished cooking and ready to put your skillet away. Cast iron skillets should be stored in a warm, dry place, such as a gas oven that has a pilot light.

Bronzing

The method for bronzing is similar to that for blackening except that the pan should be heated only to 350°, which takes about 4 minutes, and you don't have to use a cast iron skillet. Bronzing can be done indoors. Because the temperature is lower, you'll cook each piece of fish (or bird or meat) a little longer. Watch the first fillet you cook, and determine the best time for the variety you're bronzing.

The key to bronzing is to keep the skillet as close to 350° as possible, a simple matter if you use an electric skillet or a skillet thermometer, called a GrilleTemp™, available at kitchen gadget shops. You can still judge the approximate temperature even if you're bronzing with a skillet on the stove. If the temperature drops too low, which will produce less taste and more dryness, you'll notice that the food cooks very slowly. When bronzing is done properly at 350°, it cooks about as fast as it would if there were oil in the skillet. If the temperature rises too far above 350°, blue smoke will rise, which indicates that the temperature is too high for bronzing.

So remember:

DO NOT OVERCOOK! DO NOT OVERSEASON!

Blackening and Bronzing Table

Blackened Redfish Magic, Seafood Magic, or Meat Magic	Redfish, pompano, red snapper fillets, salmon steaks, or any firm-fleshed fish, about ½ to ¾ inch thick
Blackened Steak Magic or Meat Magic	Prime rib, sirloin steak, ribeye, porterhouse, filet mignon, about 1 inch thick; hamburgers (ground meat, chuck, sirloin), about ¾ to 1 inch thick
Pork and Veal Magic or Meat Magic	Pork chops, veal chops, lamb chops, about ¾ to 1 inch thick
Poultry Magic or Meat Magic	Chicken or turkey, boned and pounded flat to ½ inch thick

Blackened Steak

You can't imagine how exciting beef can taste until you bite into a blackened steak! Don't misunderstand—I have nothing against charcoal broiling, but the crust that blackening gives a steak just can't be duplicated with any other cooking method, and I think it adds a whole new dimension to the taste of the meat. Let me explain what I mean. Blackening uses extremely high, perfectly dry heat, which causes some very real changes in the surface of the meat. This high, dry heat physically alters the meat's structure, adding sweetness and yet a taste of acidity, as well as a roasted flavor. This changed surface of the meat produces a contrast to the flavor of the meat's interior, yet it's a natural progression of flavor, and it's the combination of these two tastes that makes the blackened meat (or fowl or fish) so delicious. A similar combination can be achieved by adding a good sauce, but where the sauce is made from other ingredients, the flavor produced by the blackened surface is naturally related to the inside portion of the food.

The procedure is very simple if you follow directions. Interestingly enough, I've often found that home cooks do this better than professionals because home cooks follow the directions to the last detail, whereas professionals sometimes let what they know interfere with what they see in the recipe, and therefore they may miss the mark ever so slightly.

Blackening, like charcoal broiling, must be done outside or in a commercial restaurant kitchen.

4 tablespoons (½ stick) unsalted butter, melted and slightly cooled
6 steaks (prime rib, sirloin, ribeye, porterhouse, or filet mignon), each about 1 inch thick, at room temperature
1 tablespoon Chef Paul Prudhomme's Blackened Steak Magic® or Chef Paul Prudhomme's Meat Magic®

Heat a large cast iron skillet over very high heat until it is extremely hot, at least 500°. It will take about 10 minutes to reach that temperature.

Brush one side of each steak with melted butter, then evenly sprinkle ¼ teaspoon Blackened Steak Magic (or Meat Magic) on the buttered side of each steak. Place the steaks in the hot skillet, buttered and seasoned sides down. Brush the top sides of the steaks with butter and evenly sprinkle each steak with the remaining seasoning, and cook, turning frequently, until the steaks cook to the desired doneness. Be careful not to cook too long. Serve piping hot.

If you find it necessary to cook the steaks in batches because of the size of your skillet, clean the skillet after each batch by quickly wiping it out with a clean, dry cloth. Bring the skillet back to the extreme high heat before cooking the remaining steaks. Wiping out the skillet between batches will help eliminate a burned taste. After the second batch, the skillet should be burned out by inverting the skillet over an open flame for about 3 to 5 minutes, then wiping with a heavy cloth until the skillet looks clean and no large particles continue to appear on the cloth. Then, before continuing to cook, use a fresh cloth with a small amount of oil on it to wipe the skillet one more time. Use this same procedure—burning out, wiping until clean, then wiping with the lightly oiled clean cloth—when you are finished cooking and ready to put your skillet away. Cast iron skillets should be stored in a warm, dry place, such as a gas oven that has a pilot light.

That's it! Because the method is simple, any variation will make a dramatic difference. Be sure the skillet is hot enough, and absolutely dry. Be sure not to overseason—the seasoning should highlight the taste, rather than hide it. And you don't want to overcook the steaks—there's a big difference between blackened and burned. You don't want a bitter, harsh, ashy taste. We recommend cooking no higher than medium—never well done—because the longer you cook the meat, the dryer it will become.

If you must use cold meat, you will have to adjust the cooking time and turn the steaks almost constantly to avoid burning. If you want a low fat dish, you'll be glad to know that blackening can be done without butter or oil. Simply omit the butter and use the same skillet you would if you were using butter. You also can start the steaks in the skillet for the blackened coating that you want, then finish them in the oven.

Bronzed Fish

Bronzing, which can be done indoors, is a versatile technique that works well on almost any firm fish, so experiment with seasonings and cooking times and try it with several varieties, such as tilapia, trout, redfish, red snapper, orange roughy, or tuna. Try to find fillets that are uniform in thickness, so they will cook evenly.

2 tablespoons (¼ stick) unsalted butter, melted and slightly cooled
6 (4 to 5 ounces each) fresh fish fillets, at room temperature

1 tablespoon Chef Paul Prudhomme's Blackened Redfish Magic®, Chef Paul Prudhomme's Seafood Magic® or Chef Paul Prudhomme's Meat Magic®

Heat a 10-inch skillet, preferably nonstick, over high heat to 350°, about 4 minutes.

Be sure the fish is at room temperature, so that the butter will adhere but not congeal. Brush one side of each fillet with the melted butter and evenly sprinkle ¼ teaspoon Blackened Redfish Magic or Seafood Magic or Meat Magic on the buttered side of each fillet. Carefully place the fillets, two at a time, buttered and seasoned sides down, in the skillet. Brush the top side of each fillet with butter and evenly sprinkle each side with ¼ teaspoon Blackened Redfish Magic or Seafood Magic or Meat Magic. Reduce the heat to medium and cook, turning several times, to the desired doneness. To test for doneness, at the thickest part of the fish, try to flake it with a fork. If it does flake, it's done, so remove it immediately. If it doesn't flake, cook just a little longer and test again. Be careful not to overcook or the fish will be too dry. Wipe out the skillet, bring it back to 350°, and repeat with the remaining fillets. Serve piping hot.

If you must use cold fish, you will have to adjust the cooking time and turn the fillets almost continuously to avoid burning. If you want a low-fat dish, you'll be glad to know that bronzing can be done without butter or oil. Simply omit the butter and use the same skillet you would if you were using butter.

Chef Paul Prudhomme's Kitchen Expedition ❀ 51

Photograph No. 1 Marinated Artichokes, Fried Oysters and Magic Dipping Sauce

Photograph No. 2 Crawfish and Cilantro Slats

Photograph No. 3 (Clockwise from upper left) Crab Bisque, Fire-Roasted Pearl Onion Soup, Uncle Sy's Chicken Soup, and Choleta's Yucca Chips

Photograph No. 4 Salmon Salad on Cassava Crispies

Photograph No. 5 Sirloin Steak Roulades, Pico de Gallo

Photograph No. 6 Meatballs with an Herbal Tomato Sauce

Photograph No. 7 Roasted Pork Tenderloin with Rosemary Potatoes

Photograph No. 8 Chicken with Sweet and Sour Cabbage

<u>Photograph No. 9</u> Tasso-Stuffed White Squash (background), Game Hens Stuffed with Italian Sausage, and Kohlrabi Rice (foreground)

Photograph No. 10 Bronzed Trout with a Mango-Spinach Purée,
Honey-Mustard Corn Chow-Chow

Photograph No. 11 Salmon Pudding with a Portobello Glaze

Photograph No. 12 French Quarter Eggplant

Photograph No. 13 Butternut Squash and Spinach Lasagna

Photograph No. 14 Tricolor Vegetable Terrine and
Roasted Pepper Sauce

Photograph No. 15 White Chocolate and Cheese Custard
and Berry Sauce

WHERE'S YOUR BEEF?

Sirloin Steak Roulades

Photograph No. 5

MAKES 6 SERVINGS

Roulade is the French word for something that's rolled up, usually around some kind of stuffing. Most often it's thin pieces of meat, but it can refer to crêpes or sponge cake, such as in jelly rolls. Here we're talking about thin sirloin steaks rolled around a colorful and delicious vegetable filling, browned, then simmered in a great sauce. Get out of the way, Papa's coming home for dinner!

You can cut the steaks yourself or you can have the butcher do it for you, but the most important thing, after the quality of the meat, is to buy the thinnest steak you can find. When you pound the pieces, it's a good idea to place them between layers of heavy plastic wrap—this makes the task a little neater, and it keeps bits of meat from sticking in the crevices of the mallet. Instead of using oil to cook the roulades, you can spray them with vegetable oil spray and cook them in a dry non-stick skillet. Also, you can use 2¼ cups chopped bell peppers of any color instead of buying three different-colored peppers. It's important for the mango to be really ripe, or it won't add the expected sweetness.

SEASONING MIX

2½ teaspoons salt
1¼ teaspoons garlic powder
1¼ teaspoons ground ginger
1¼ teaspoons onion powder
1¼ teaspoons paprika
1¼ teaspoons ground dried Anaheim
    chile peppers (see pages 1 and 2)

1 teaspoon cayenne
1 teaspoon dry mustard
1 teaspoon ground dried guajillo
    chile peppers (see pages 1 and 2)
1 teaspoon dried thyme leaves
¾ teaspoon black pepper
½ teaspoon white pepper

2 pounds thin sirloin steak, cut
    into 6 narrow, equal slices,
    about 5 ounces each
4 tablespoons vegetable oil, in all
1½ cups chopped onions, about 1
    medium
¾ cup chopped green bell peppers,
    about ¾ medium
¾ cup chopped red bell peppers,
    about ¾ medium
¾ cup chopped yellow bell
    peppers, about ¾ medium

1½ cups white potatoes, peeled
    and diced into ½-inch cubes,
    about 1 medium (10 ounces)
1½ cups beef stock (see page 6)
1½ cups ripe mango (see page
    168), peeled, pitted, and diced
    into ½-inch cubes, about 1
    medium-size
½ cup unseasoned bread crumbs
1 (15-ounce) can diced tomatoes
    (see page 7)

Combine the seasoning mix ingredients in a small bowl and mix well.

With a tenderizing mallet, pound out the steak pieces until very thin. Sprinkle each side of each steak evenly with ½ teaspoon seasoning mix and rub it in well.

In a 4-quart pot over high heat, heat 2 tablespoons of the oil just until it begins to smoke, about 3 to 4 minutes. Add the onions, bell peppers, potatoes, and the remaining seasoning mix. Cover and cook for 15 minutes. Uncover, stir and scrape thoroughly and add the stock and mango. Re-cover and cook, stirring every 2 or 3 minutes, for 15 minutes, then remove from the heat. You should have about 3 cups of stuffing. Remove and set aside half of this mixture to make the sauce.

To the mixture remaining in the pot, add the bread crumbs and mix them in well—now you've made the stuffing! Divide this stuffing evenly among the 6 steaks, placing it along the center of each steak. Tuck the ends in and roll the steaks up—the finished roulades should be shaped like large egg rolls. Secure with toothpicks or clean cotton string.

In a 12-inch skillet over high heat, heat the remaining 2 tablespoons oil for 3 minutes and brown the roulades on all sides, about 10 minutes. While the roulades are browning, add the reserved stuffing to the skillet and stir it every 2 minutes. Remove the roulades when they are browned and add the tomatoes to the skillet. Stir well to combine and cook the sauce for 8 minutes. Return the roulades to the skillet and lower the heat to medium. Simmer, turning the roulades every 5 minutes, until the meat is tender, about 20 to 25 minutes, depending upon the thickness of the meat. Serve hot with buttered broad noodles.

Barbecue Meat Loaf with a Sauce

MAKES 8 SERVINGS

What makes this different from other barbecue recipes is the combination of cumin and chipotle chiles with the hickory flavor. If you can't find powdered hickory smoke, you can substitute the same amount of bottled liquid smoke flavoring, and add it along with the eggs. A helpful hint when making meat loaf is to be careful not to overmix; overmixing releases the protein in the meat and makes it mushy. Mixing it to death kills the taste too, so blend no longer than necessary to distribute the ingredients. I think this meat loaf is great with oven-roasted whole potatoes, turnips and onions, and it's terrific the next day. Sliced and either cold or reheated, it makes really good sandwiches, using the sauce, which was developed after we finished taping the television show, instead of ketchup. Have you ever tried frying a slice of meat loaf? It's so good it's worth making sure you have some left over.

SEASONING MIX

1 tablespoon plus 1½ teaspoons salt
1 tablespoon dried basil leaves
1 tablespoon ground cumin
1 tablespoon ground ginger
1 tablespoon powdered hickory
    smoke (preferred, or bottled
    liquid smoke to add later)
2½ teaspoons garlic powder

2¼ teaspoons dry mustard
2¼ teaspoons onion powder
2 teaspoons cayenne
1½ teaspoons ground dill seeds
1½ teaspoons black pepper
1½ teaspoons ground dried chipotle
    chile peppers (see pages 1 and 2)
¾ teaspoon white pepper

1½ cups chopped onions, about 1
    medium
½ cup chopped green bell peppers,
    about ½ medium
½ cup chopped red bell peppers,
    about ½ medium
½ cup chopped yellow bell
    peppers, about ½ medium
¾ cup chopped celery, about 2
    small stalks

1½ cups chopped ripe fresh
    tomatoes (see page 7)
1 tablespoon minced fresh garlic
1 tablespoon minced fresh ginger
½ cup ketchup
2 large eggs, lightly beaten
¾ cup unseasoned bread crumbs
2 pounds ground beef

Combine the seasoning mix ingredients in a small bowl and mix well.

Preheat a heavy 4-quart pot over high heat until very hot, about 4 minutes. Add the onions, bell peppers, celery, and 2 tablespoons of the seasoning mix. Cook, stirring and scraping the bottom of the pot once a minute, until the vegetables are sticking hard, about 5 minutes.

Add the tomatoes, garlic, ginger, and 5 tablespoons of the seasoning mix. Scrape the pan well and cook, scraping every 2 to 3 minutes, until the mixture again sticks hard to the bottom of the pot and the crust on the bottom is difficult to scrape up, about 10 minutes. I know this sounds like a lot of scraping and sticking hard, but we want the vegetables to be somewhat caramelized, to brown and develop their starches, which produces a great natural sweetness—they should be dark and look pasty. Remove from the heat, stir in the ketchup, and set aside to cool.

Preheat the oven to 350°.

Whip the eggs and stir them (and the bottled liquid smoke flavoring, if using) into the cooled vegetable mixture. Fold this mixture and the bread crumbs into the ground meat, combining all the ingredients thoroughly but gently, and place in a 5-inch by 9-inch by 4-inch metal loaf pan. Bake until the interior of the meat loaf reaches 150° (use a meat thermometer and be sure it doesn't touch any part of the pan), about 1 hour. While the meat loaf is baking make the sauce (recipe follows). When the meat loaf is done, remove it from the oven, pour off the pan drippings, and let it sit for 5 to 10 minutes before slicing. Serve with the Barbecue Sauce.

Barbecue Sauce

MAKES 5 CUPS

2 tablespoons vegetable oil
1½ cups chopped onions, about 1 medium
1 cup chopped celery, about 1 stalk
1 cup fresh grapefruit juice
1 (15-ounce) can tomato purée
1 cup tomato sauce
¼ cup ketchup
¼ cup lightly packed dark brown sugar
2 tablespoons cane vinegar (see page 172)
1 cup chicken stock (see page 5)
2 tablespoons cane syrup (see page 165)
2 bay leaves

In a 2-quart pot over high heat, heat the oil just until it begins to smoke, about 3 to 4 minutes. Add the onions, celery, and the remaining seasoning mix. Cook, stirring and scraping the pot every 1 or 2 minutes, until the vegetables begin to stick hard to the bottom of the pot, about 8 minutes. Stir in the grapefruit juice and scrape up the brown bits from the bottom and sides of the pot. Cook, stirring constantly, for 2 more minutes, then add the tomato purée, tomato sauce, ketchup, brown sugar, vinegar, stock, cane syrup, and bay leaves. Bring to a boil, stirring every 1 or 2 minutes, then reduce the heat to low and simmer for 30 minutes. Remove from the heat and serve.

Beef Short Ribs Roasted "Golden" Style

MAKES 4 TO 6 SERVINGS

Golden Williams, a cameraman at WYES, the New Orleans public television station where the Kitchen Expedition *series was videotaped, liked these ribs so much we just had to name them for him. Enjoy, Golden, you're a great example of the kind of appetite I like to see!*

As you can tell from just looking at the recipe, these ribs are easy to prepare! And oh, are they delicious! I have to admit the seasoning is peppery, so if you prefer less heat, reduce the amount of cayenne and ground chile peppers. When you're shopping, be sure to buy ribs with plenty of layers of fat, so the meat will stay juicy during the long, slow cooking. This recipe is great for entertaining, because once you get them in the oven, you don't have to tend to the ribs—you can devote your full attention to your guests, and you can all enjoy the heavenly fragrance coming from the oven. If you like, serve these with our Barbecue Sauce, page 57.

SEASONING MIX

2 teaspoons paprika
2 teaspoons salt
1½ teaspoons dried basil leaves
1 teaspoon cayenne
1 teaspoon garlic powder
1 teaspoon onion powder
1 teaspoon ground dried árbol chile
    peppers (see pages 1 and 2)

1 teaspoon ground dried Anaheim
    chile peppers (see pages 1 and 2)
¾ teaspoon black pepper
¾ teaspoon ground savory
½ teaspoon dry mustard
½ teaspoon white pepper

4½ pounds beef short ribs

Preheat the oven to 275°.

Combine the seasoning mix ingredients in a small bowl and mix well.

Sprinkle all the seasoning mix evenly over all sides of the ribs and gently rub it in. Place the ribs in a large roasting pan or divide them between 2 pans if necessary, but you don't need a rack. Roast the ribs, enjoying the terrific aroma all the while, until the meat is tender and falls off the bone, about 3 to 4 hours, depending upon the size of the ribs. Serve hot with plenty of paper napkins.

Flank Steak Scallops with Plantains and Pasta

MAKES 4 SERVINGS

We scallop the steak to create additional meat surface, which allows more of the seasonings to flavor it. The technique, described on page 4, is not at all difficult, and produces some of the most tender meat you'll ever enjoy. The ginger and plantains add a great touch of sweetness, and the jalapeño chile peppers spark the dish with just the right amount of heat. If you want to make this delicious dinner really colorful, you can use tri-color pasta, and serve it with julienne strips of brilliantly-colored vegetables, blanched for just a minute or two so they'll keep their color.

SEASONING MIX

2 teaspoons salt
1 teaspoon cayenne
1 teaspoon ground cumin
1 teaspoon garlic powder
1 teaspoon ground ginger
1 teaspoon onion powder

¾ teaspoon ground coriander
¾ teaspoon dry mustard
½ teaspoon ground allspice
¼ teaspoon ground mace
¼ teaspoon black pepper
¼ teaspoon white pepper

1½ pounds flank steak, scalloped
  (see page 4)
4 tablespoons olive oil, in all
2 cups chopped onions, about 1
  medium (10 ounces)
3 cups very ripe plantains, peeled
  and diced into ¼-inch pieces,
  about 2 medium-size

1 tablespoon minced fresh ginger
¼ cup minced fresh jalapeño chile
  peppers (see pages 1 and 2)
1 teaspoon minced fresh garlic
3 cups beef stock (see page 6)
1 cup heavy cream
4 cups cooked pasta

Combine the seasoning mix ingredients in a small bowl and mix well.

Sprinkle the meat evenly with 2 tablespoons of the seasoning mix and rub it in well.

Heat 2 tablespoons of the oil in a heavy 12-inch nonstick skillet over high heat until it begins to smoke, about 3 to 4 minutes. Add the beef scallops, one layer at a time (don't overcrowd the skillet) and brown them on both sides. Remove the first batch from the pan and repeat the process until all the meat is browned.

To the same skillet add the remaining oil, the onions, plantains, ginger, jalapeño peppers, garlic, and remaining seasoning mix. Cook, stirring and scraping the skillet bottom every 3 minutes, until the plantains begin to break up and the mixture starts to brown, about 10 minutes. Add the stock and scrape up the brown bits on the skillet bottom, breaking up the plantains and whisking them into the liquid to help thicken the sauce. Bring to a boil, then whisk in the cream. Return just to a boil, return the meat and its accumulated juices to the skillet, and simmer for 3 minutes. Remove from the heat, add the pasta, stir until it's thoroughly warmed, and serve.

Ten-Chile Meat Loaf

MAKES 6 TO 8 SERVINGS

Ten—count 'em—ten different kinds of chile peppers! I give you fair warning: this meat loaf is hot enough to curl your toenails. If you don't like so much heat, cut down on the amount of ground chiles. Don't reduce the number of different chiles, just reduce the quantity of each one, so you'll still have a balanced, complex taste. If you can't find the fresh Anaheim or jalapeño chile peppers where you shop, substitute an equal amount of canned chiles. If you're sensitive to the capsicum (the hot stuff) in chiles or if you have a cut on your hand, I suggest you wear plastic or latex gloves to do the mixing, since there are so many chiles, both dried and fresh. I like the way the three colors of bell peppers look in this meat loaf, but you can use three cups of all one color if you prefer.

A helpful hint when making meat loaf is to be careful not to overmix; overmixing releases the protein in the meat and makes it mushy. Mixing it to death kills the taste too, so blend no longer than necessary to distribute the ingredients.

SEASONING MIX

1 tablespoon plus ½ teaspoon salt
2 teaspoons dry mustard
2 teaspoons paprika
2 teaspoons ground dried New Mexico chile peppers (see pages 1 and 2)
1¾ teaspoons ground dried Anaheim chile peppers (see pages 1 and 2)
1½ teaspoons ground cumin
1½ teaspoons garlic powder

1½ teaspoons ground ginger
1½ teaspoons onion powder
1½ teaspoons dried oregano leaves
1 teaspoon cayenne
1 teaspoon ground dried árbol chile peppers (see pages 1 and 2)
¾ teaspoon black pepper
¾ teaspoon ground dried ancho chile peppers (see pages 1 and 2)
½ teaspoon white pepper

1 cup unseasoned bread crumbs
2 tablespoons olive oil
2 cups chopped onions
1 cup chopped green bell peppers, about 1 medium
1 cup chopped red bell pepper, about 1 medium
1 cup chopped yellow bell peppers, about 1 medium
1 cup chopped fresh Anaheim chile peppers (see pages 1 and 2)

1 cup chopped fresh jalapeño chile peppers (see pages 1 and 2)
2 cups sweet potatoes, peeled and diced into ¼-inch cubes
1 tablespoon minced fresh garlic, about 3 cloves
2 tablespoons minced fresh ginger
2 (4.5-ounce) cans diced mild green chilies
1 pound ground pork
1 pound ground beef
2 large eggs, lightly beaten

Combine the seasoning mix ingredients in a small bowl and mix well.

Toast the bread crumbs in a small skillet over high heat, stirring and shaking constantly to prevent burning, until they are the color of light peanut butter and give off a toasty aroma, about 5 minutes. Immediately remove the bread crumbs from the skillet to stop the toasting and set aside.

In a heavy 12-inch skillet, preferably nonstick, over high heat, heat the oil just until it begins to smoke, about 3 to 4 minutes. Add the onions, bell peppers, Anaheim chiles, jalapeños, sweet potatoes, and 3 tablespoons of the seasoning mix. Stir well, then cover and cook, uncovering to stir every 3 to 4 minutes, for 15 minutes. Uncover and add the garlic, ginger, canned chiles, and the remaining seasoning mix. Re-cover and cook, uncovering to stir at 2-minute intervals, for 4 to 6 minutes. Uncover and cook, stirring and scraping up the brown crust on the bottom of the skillet almost constantly as the mixture thickens and starts to stick, about 10 minutes longer. Remove from the heat and cool.

Combine the pork, beef, eggs, bread crumbs, and vegetable mixture. Mix with your hands just until combined (for the best texture and flavor, be careful not to overmix), then place into a 9-inch by 5-inch by 4-inch loaf pan. Bake until the internal temperature of the loaf reaches 150° (insert a meat thermometer halfway into the meat loaf, and be sure it doesn't touch the pan), about 1½ hours. Remove the meat loaf from the pan or pour off the pan drippings, and let sit for 5 to 10 minutes before serving.

Standing Rib Roast with a Pepper Cap

MAKES 8 SERVINGS

Because the heat of fresh chile peppers varies according to the season and region where they're grown, taste them before you make the pepper cap to be sure it's not going to be too hot. To do this, cut the end off the pepper and lightly touch it to the middle of your tongue. If it's too hot, reduce the quantity or use another pepper.

The dried and fresh chile peppers plus the fresh ginger are what make this roast stand out from those I've done before. The pepper cap is loaded with flavor, but according to Sean O'Meara, who works with me in the test kitchen, once you've got the degree of heat the way you want it, friends or family members can always scrape it off if they must! For those who can stand the heat, though, this roast is just about perfect. It looks great, will impress your guests, and tastes like more. As a matter of fact, if you're lucky enough to have any left over, it makes fabulous sandwiches.

SEASONING MIX

2 teaspoons garlic powder
2 teaspoons onion powder
2 teaspoons paprika
2 teaspoons ground dried chipotle
    chile peppers (see pages 1 and 2)
2 teaspoons salt
2 teaspoons dried thyme leaves
1½ teaspoons cayenne
1½ teaspoons ground coriander

1½ teaspoons black pepper
1 teaspoon ground allspice
1 teaspoon dry mustard
1 teaspoon white pepper
1 teaspoon ground dried New Mexico
    chile peppers (see pages 1 and 2)
1 teaspoon ground dried ancho chile
    peppers (see pages 1 and 2)

2 tablespoons olive oil
3 cups chopped onions, about 2
    medium
1 cup chopped green bell peppers,
    about 1 medium
1 cup chopped red bell peppers,
    about 1 medium
1 cup chopped yellow bell peppers,
    about 1 medium
2 cups chopped celery, about 2 stalks
3 tablespoons minced fresh garlic,
    about 9 cloves
3 tablespoons minced fresh ginger
1½ cups fresh poblano chile peppers
    (see pages 1 and 2), diced into
    ¼-inch pieces

½ cup fresh jalapeño chile peppers
    (see pages 1 and 2), diced into
    ¼-inch pieces
¼ cup fresh serrano chile peppers
    (see pages 1 and 2), diced into
    ¼-inch pieces
½ cup beef stock (see page 6)
¼ cup cane syrup (see page 165),
    preferred, or pure maple syrup
1 cup loosely packed cilantro leaves
1 standing rib roast (about 8 to 9
    pounds, 4 ribs), trimmed of
    excess fat

Combine the seasoning mix ingredients in a small bowl and mix well.

In a heavy 4-quart pot over high heat, heat the oil just until it begins to smoke, about 3 to 4 minutes. Add the onions, bell peppers, and celery. Cook, stirring every 3 to 4 minutes, for 15 minutes, then add the garlic, ginger, chile peppers, and 3 tablespoons of the seasoning mix. Cook, stirring and scraping every 3 or 4 minutes, until the mixture sticks hard to the bottom of the pot, about 10 minutes. Stir in the stock and scrape well. Cook for 5 minutes then add the cane syrup and cilantro. Cook, stirring every 4 or 5 minutes, until the mixture is well browned, about 10 minutes. Remove all but 1½ cups of the mixture (which will be used for the sauce) from the pot and set it aside to stuff the roast.

Preheat the oven to 300°.

Cut pockets in the top of the roast, about 1 inch deep and ¾ inch apart. Season the top of the roast evenly with the remaining seasoning mix, working some into the pockets by putting small amounts on a teaspoon, opening the pockets, and shoving it into the pockets with your fingers until they're full. Rub the remaining seasoning mix across the top of the roast, then spread the reserved vegetable mixture evenly over the top of the seasoned roast. Place the roast in a large roasting pan, standing up so that it's resting on its rack of ribs, which allows the fat to melt and baste the meat. Roast until the internal temperature of the meat reaches 125° (insert a meat thermometer into the roast, being sure that it doesn't touch any of the bones or the pan), about 3 hours. Reserve the pan drippings, discarding the excess fat, for the sauce (recipe below).

SAUCE

1½ cups vegetable mixture remaining in the pot
Drippings from the roasting pan
2 tablespoons all-purpose flour

4 cups beef stock (see page 6)
2 tablespoons Worcestershire sauce
¼ teaspoon salt

Re-heat the vegetable mixture, along with the reserved pan drippings, in the pot for 4 minutes. Whisk in the flour until it is completely absorbed, then whisk in the stock, Worcestershire sauce, and salt. Bring just to a boil, reduce the heat to low and simmer, whisking every 4 or 5 minutes, until the sauce is thick and rich, about 15 minutes. To serve, slice the roast, drizzle each slice with some of the sauce, and pass the rest of the sauce separately.

Meatballs with an Herbal Tomato Sauce

Photograph No. 6

MAKES 8 GENEROUS SERVINGS

It's unlikely you've ever tasted meatballs like these before! Not only are they baked rather than fried, they're made of more than just meat—they're packed with a spicy vegetable purée and topped with a taste-tempting sauce fairly bursting with more luscious ripe vegetables. If you're counting calories, you can reduce or omit the olive oil in this recipe, but you'll lose that wonderful flavor. If you can't find serrano peppers, you can use any moderately hot chile pepper.

SEASONING MIX

2½ teaspoons salt
2 teaspoons paprika
1½ teaspoons dried oregano leaves
1 teaspoon dried basil leaves
1 teaspoon garlic powder
1 teaspoon ground ginger
1 teaspoon dry mustard

1 teaspoon onion powder
1 teaspoon ground dried ancho chile
    peppers (see pages 1 and 2)
¾ teaspoon black pepper
½ teaspoon cayenne
¼ teaspoon white pepper

Up to 6 tablespoons olive oil, in all
2 (15-ounce) cans tomato sauce, in all
2½ cups chopped onions, about 2
    medium, in all
2 cups chopped green bell peppers,
    about 2 medium, in all
1 cup chopped red bell peppers, about
    1 medium
1 cup chopped yellow bell peppers,
    about 1 medium
2 tablespoons minced fresh garlic,
    about 6 cloves
2 tablespoons minced fresh thyme
    leaves, in all

2 tablespoons minced fresh oregano
    leaves, in all
½ teaspoon salt
2 (15-ounce) cans diced tomatoes (see
    page 7)
2 cups beef stock or chicken stock (see
    pages 5 and 6)
1 pound ground beef
1 large egg, lightly beaten
2 tablespoons minced fresh serrano
    chile peppers (see pages 1 and 2)
½ cup unseasoned bread crumbs
Flour for dusting
2 tablespoons firmly packed dark
    brown sugar

Combine the seasoning mix ingredients in a small bowl and mix well.

To start the sauce, you have a choice—either heat up to 2 tablespoons of the olive oil in a 6-inch skillet, or preheat the empty skillet over high heat until it's very hot, about 4 minutes. Add 1 can of the tomato sauce and, as soon as the sauce begins to sputter, reduce the heat to low and cover. Cook, carefully uncovering to stir every 5 minutes, until most of the liquid evaporates and the sauce is thick and dark red brown, about 40 minutes to 1 hour. Remove from the heat, uncover, and continue to stir every 2 to 3 minutes until the mixture has stopped cooking, that is, when the sauce has thickened and is a dark brick-red color. Set aside.

Heat up to 4 tablespoons (¼ cup) of olive oil in a 10-inch skillet over high heat just until it begins to smoke, about 3 to 4 minutes. Add 1½ cups of the onions, 1 cup of the green bell peppers, the red and yellow bell peppers, and the seasoning mix. Cover and cook, stirring every 4 to 5 minutes at first, then more frequently as the vegetables brown and begin to stick, for 15 minutes. Remove from the heat. Remove 1 cup of the mixture, purée it, and refrigerate until cold, about 15 minutes. Reserve the mixture remaining in the pot for the sauce.

Place a 4-quart pot over high heat and add the reserved vegetable mixture, the remaining green bell peppers, the remaining onions, the garlic, 1 tablespoon of the thyme, 1 tablespoon of the oregano, the salt, diced tomatoes, the browned tomato sauce, the remaining can of tomato sauce, and the stock. Bring just to a boil, then reduce the heat to medium and simmer briskly, stirring every 5 minutes, for 40 minutes. While the sauce is simmering, make the meatballs.

If you're able to work without interruptions, the timing should come out just about right—the meatballs will come out of the oven just at the end of the 40 minutes of simmering. If, however, the meatballs are done first, simply remove them from the oven and set them aside until you add them to the sauce, and if the 40 minutes are over before the meatballs are done, just remove the sauce from the heat, cover and set it aside, then re-heat it when the meatballs are ready.

Preheat the oven to 350°.

In a large bowl, combine the beef, the cold puréed vegetables, the egg, serrano chile peppers, and bread crumbs and mix gently but thoroughly. Wear thin latex or plastic gloves to shape the meatballs if you're sensitive to chiles. Shape heaping tablespoons of the mixture into 1½-inch diameter meatballs—you should have about 40—roll them lightly in flour, then place on a lightly floured cookie sheet. Bake until the meatballs are golden brown, about 10 to 12 minutes.

With the sauce simmering briskly over medium heat, stir in the remaining thyme and oregano, add the brown sugar and meatballs, and simmer briskly for 5 minutes. Stir and scrape the pot bottom thoroughly, then cook for 5 minutes longer. Remove from the heat and serve immediately over your favorite pasta.

Flour Tortilla Rolls
with Steak and Vegetables

MAKES 12 SERVINGS

When we were taste-testing the recipes for this book, nobody didn't like this one! The components look familiar to you, but one bite will let you know there's something different going on here. Besides the chile peppers for a gentle nudge of heat and the cumin that you'd expect in a recipe with Mexican ancestry, we've jazzed it up with dry mustard and ground ginger, and we start off with sirloin steak! Choose a well-marbled steak, for those thin streaks of fat running through the meat enhance its flavor, tenderness, and juiciness.

This is a recipe that lends itself to entertaining because much of the preparation can be done ahead. Cook and slice the steak, cut the vegetables and store them in plastic zipper bags, and get the avocado dressing and Pico de Gallo (see page 48) ready at your convenience. Then, when your guests are ready to dig in, assemble the rolls and serve them, or let each person fix his own. By the way, the vegetable mixture is great in an omelet!

SEASONING MIX

2 teaspoons paprika
2 teaspoons salt
1¼ teaspoons ground cumin
1¼ teaspoons dry mustard
1¼ teaspoons onion powder
1 teaspoon ground dried Anaheim
    chile peppers (see pages 1 and 2)

¾ teaspoon garlic powder
¾ teaspoon ground ginger
¾ teaspoon ground dried árbol chile
    peppers (see pages 1 and 2)
½ teaspoon cayenne
½ teaspoon black pepper
½ teaspoon white pepper

1 (1½- to 2-pound) sirloin steak
2 teaspoons sugar
1 green bell pepper, cut into
    ½-inch wide julienne strips (see
    page 3)
1 red bell pepper, cut into ½-inch
    wide julienne strips (see page 3)
1 yellow bell pepper, cut into
    ½-inch wide julienne strips (see
    page 3)
1 onion, cut into ½-inch wide
    julienne strips (see page 3)

2 tablespoons vegetable oil, plus
    additional oil for frying
2 medium-size ripe avocados,
    pitted, peeled, and sliced
1 cup sour cream (see page 3)
2 tablespoons orange juice
2 tablespoons orange zest
4 tablespoons minced fresh
    jalapeño chile peppers (see
    pages 1 and 2)
½ cup minced green onions, about
    6 stalks
12 (10-inch) flour tortillas

Combine the seasoning mix ingredients in a small bowl and mix well.

Sprinkle each side of the steak with 2 tablespoons of the seasoning mix. Combine the remaining seasoning mix with the sugar, mix well, and set aside.

Preheat a 10-inch cast iron skillet over high heat until very hot, about 8 minutes. Place the seasoned steak in the skillet and cook, turning once, until both sides are seared, about 6 to 8 minutes per side. Set aside to cool.

When the steak is cool enough to handle, slice it in half lengthwise with the grain, then slice each half into very thin slices, working against the grain. You should have about 65 strips.

VEGETABLES In a medium-size bowl or plastic zipper bag combine the onions, bell peppers, 2 tablespoons vegetable oil, and 1 tablespoon plus 1 teaspoon of the seasoning mix. Stir gently to coat the vegetables with the oil and seasonings, and set aside to marinate, stirring (or if using the plastic bag, simply turning over) about every 15 minutes, for at least 1 hour.

AVOCADO DRESSING In a medium-size bowl mash the avocados slightly (not too much, as you want them to remain slightly chunky) with a fork and add the sour cream, jalapeños, green onions, orange juice, zest, and the remaining seasoning mix. Mix lightly with a fork just until combined.

ASSEMBLY Drain the vegetables and discard the marinade.

Preheat a 10-inch cast iron skillet over high heat until very hot, about 8 minutes. Add 1 tablespoon oil and cook ¼ of the vegetable strips, stirring constantly, just until the vegetables are beginning to brown along the edges, 1 to 2 minutes. Remove these vegetables from the skillet and add a little more oil if necessary. Repeat the steps with the remaining vegetables.

Pour enough oil into a large skillet to measure 2 inches deep, and heat it to 350°. Use a cooking thermometer and adjust the heat to keep the oil as close to 350° as possible. An electric skillet, if you have one, works great.

Preheat another clean 10-inch skillet to medium hot, about 3 minutes. Soften a tortilla by placing it in the hot dry skillet, turning frequently, for about 20 seconds. Remove the tortilla from the skillet and place 3 tablespoons of the avocado mixture in a long rectangular shape near an edge of the tortilla, and top the avocado with 5 strips of the meat and 1 strip of each vegetable. Fold the near edge of the tortilla fairly firmly over the fillings and roll the filled tortilla over an inch or so. Tuck in the two sides of the tortilla next to the rolled section, eggroll fashion, and continue to roll up the filled tortilla. Secure with toothpicks, using as few as possible. Repeat for the remaining tortillas.

Cook the rolls, turning very frequently, in the hot oil for 3 minutes. Very quickly remove the rolls from the oil, remove and discard the toothpicks, and return the rolls to the oil. Cook, turning often, just until they are golden and crispy on all sides, about 2 to 3 minutes longer. Remove from the oil and drain on paper towels.

To serve, slice each roll through the center at a 45-degree angle. Stand up both halves on a plate and place 1 tablespoon of Pico de Gallo sauce (page 44) with each serving.

Sweetmeat Croqueseignols

MAKES ABOUT 24

I got the idea for this recipe when my van broke down on a narrow street in the Middle East. While we were waiting for repairs, I sent an associate to a nearby bakery for some snacks, and she came back with a great selection. One of the treats was a little meat pie, and its crust was as savory and delicious as its filling. I'm not trying to copy the flavors of that pastry, but it certainly did inspire me to start thinking about the possibilities!

Croqueseignols (pronounced something like crook-sin-yawls) is the Cajun-French name for doughnuts, which are generally cake-like in texture. Well, these croquesignols aren't going to remind you of doughnut shop products, but uuuuum are they good! Serve one to a person as an appetizer, or with a salad for a light lunch or supper. If you don't have the 3-inch cookie cutter or dumpling press called for, you can use a jar or glass of the right size.

Here's a hint that may save you a burn: when you uncover a pan, tilt the lid away from you so the steam doesn't get in your face. Then let the condensed liquid drop back into the pan so you don't unbalance the recipe.

1¾ teaspoons salt
1¼ teaspoons ground coriander
1¼ teaspoons ground cumin
1 teaspoon ground cardamom
1 teaspoon dry mustard
1 teaspoon onion powder
1 teaspoon paprika
1 teaspoon black pepper

¾ teaspoon garlic powder
¾ teaspoon white pepper
¾ teaspoon ground dried New
  Mexico chile peppers (see pages 1
  and 2)
¾ teaspoon ground dried pasilla
  chile peppers (see pages 1 and 2)
¾ teaspoon ground turmeric

DOUGH

6 tablespoons unsalted butter,
  melted and cooled
1 large egg
1 tablespoon plus ½ teaspoon
  baking powder
1 teaspoon dry yeast (NOT a full
  packet—measure)
1 teaspoon vanilla

¼ teaspoon salt
¼ teaspoon ground mace
¼ teaspoon ground nutmeg
¾ cup cane syrup (see page 165,
  preferred, or pure maple syrup)
¼ cup evaporated milk
3 cups all-purpose flour

FILLING

½ pound ground pork
1 teaspoon vegetable oil
½ cup chopped onions, about ½
  small (3 ounces)
1 cup Japanese eggplant,
  preferably, or standard
  eggplant, diced into ¼-inch
  cubes, about 1 Japanese
  eggplant or 1 very small
  standard eggplant

½ cup minced fresh poblano chile
  pepper (see pages 1 and 2),
  about 1 small poblano
1 cup pork stock, preferred, or beef
  stock (see page 6)
¼ cup chopped dried dates
¼ cup chopped dried figs
1 cup ripe mango (see page 168),
  peeled, seeded, and diced into
  ¼-inch cubes, about 1 small (¾
  pound) mango

1 large egg
1 tablespoon water
Vegetable oil for frying

Powdered sugar, optional, or cane
  syrup (see page 165, preferred,
  or pure maple syrup), optional

Combine the seasoning mix ingredients in a small bowl and mix well.

DOUGH In the bowl of an electric mixer equipped with a dough hook,
combine the melted butter, the egg, baking powder, yeast, vanilla, salt,
mace, nutmeg, cane syrup (or maple syrup), and evaporated milk.
Process at low speed until the ingredients are combined. Gradually
add the flour and continue to mix at low speed until it is completely

incorporated into the dough. Increase the speed to medium and process until the dough is well kneaded, about 3 minutes. Refrigerate until firm, about 1 hour.

FILLING With your hands, break up the meat into pieces as small as possible, almost granular. Because the meat is going into a small pie, you want it to be the same size as the diced vegetables.

In a 12-inch skillet over high heat, heat 1 tablespoon of the oil just until it begins to smoke, about 3 to 4 minutes. Add the onions and cook, stirring almost constantly, for 4 minutes. Add the eggplant, poblano pepper, and ½ cup stock (we're adding a little of the stock now so the eggplant will stay as moist as possible—if we fry the eggplant without this liquid, it would be too dry and not give the flavor I'm looking for in this recipe). Cover the skillet, reduce the heat to medium, and cook, stirring about once a minute (you will notice, after 3 minutes, that the mixture still has plenty of moisture), for 5 minutes. You'll see that now the mixture is getting dry (the moisture is evaporating) so we can start the browning process. Cook, uncovered, stirring every minute or so, for 5 minutes. Push the vegetables to one side of the skillet and add the meat. If this sounds too different from your way of cooking, you can remove the vegetables, brown the meat, then return the vegetables to the skillet. Sprinkle 1 tablespoon of the seasoning mix on the vegetables and 1 tablespoon seasoning mix on the meat. Continue cooking, turning the meat so all of it browns, for 5 more minutes. Stir the vegetables back into the mixture, stir and cook for 2 minutes, then add the dates, figs, and 2 teaspoons of the seasoning mix. Stir well to combine, cook for 3 minutes, then stir in 1 tablespoon seasoning mix. Cook, stirring and gently mashing the mixture, for 3 minutes, then stir in 2 teaspoons seasoning mix. Cover and cook for 1 minute, then uncover and stir in the stock (we add the stock after just a short time of cooking after adding the dates, because their sugar browns quickly and we don't want to take the chance of burning the mixture). If the mixture is very liquid, stir and cook for 1 minute longer, then remove from the heat. Stir and scrape thoroughly, mixing in the sweet, dark brown bits on the bottom of the skillet; you'll notice that these bits will soon be dissolved into the moist vegetable mixture. Gently stir in the mango and refrigerate until well chilled, about 1 hour.

Make an egg wash by beating together the egg and water. Set aside.

On a floured surface, roll out the dough to a thickness of 1/8 inch. Using a 3½-inch round cookie cutter or dumpling press, cut rounds out of the dough. Place 1 tablespoon of the meat mixture in the center of one of the rounds. Lightly paint the edges of the round with egg wash, then fold the round in half, making the shape of a turnover. Close the edges by pressing firmly with your fingers, then seal the edges using the tines of a fork. Repeat until all the rounds are filled and sealed.

These croquesignols can be steamed, baked, or fried. Each method produces a delicious meat pie, each with a very different taste. I love all three, and the steamed and baked versions are low in fat. If you can't make up your mind, try doing some of the croquesignols each way. You will be amazed by the different tastes that can come from this one recipe.

TO STEAM Place the croquesignols in a steamer—we use an Oriental one made of bamboo, but any kind will work. Cover and place over boiling water and steam until the filling is warmed through, about 8 minutes. If you don't have a steamer, you can place the croquesignols in a metal colander, cover it, and steam over a pot of boiling water—just be sure the level of the water is well below that of the little pies.

TO BAKE Preheat the oven to 350°. Place the croquesignols on a nonstick cookie sheet and bake, turning once and watching to make sure that the crust does not get too dark, until they are nicely browned, about 10 minutes.

TO FRY Into a 10-inch skillet pour enough oil to measure 1½ inches deep and heat it to 250°. Use a cooking thermometer and adjust the heat as necessary to keep the oil between 250° and 300°. If you have one, an electric skillet works well. Fry the croquesignols, turning once, until they are a dark, even brown on both sides, about 3 minutes per batch. Drain on paper towels and, if desired, top with sifted powdered sugar or cane syrup (or maple syrup). Serve hot or at room temperature.

Filet Tails with a Roasted Garlic Sauce

MAKES ABOUT 5 SERVINGS

This one-pot dish—with meat, potatoes, and carrots—is such a far cry from routine stew that we just couldn't give it such a routine name! The roasted onions and garlic give it a fire-roasted taste that is just incredible. Filet tails are the tips of the tenderloin, and are usually less expensive than the rest of the tenderloin, so order the filet tail from your butcher to make sure you don't get charged for the tenderloin cut. The tails are not always available, but you can use another good cut of beef, such as the tenderloin itself. However, the tender filet tails cook very quickly, so if you make a substitution, you'll probably have to extend the cooking time a little bit. Even though this dish contains potatoes, I like to serve it over a starch, such as more potatoes, perhaps mashed, or rice.

SEASONING MIX

2 teaspoons dried basil leaves
2 teaspoons salt
1¾ teaspoons dill weed
1½ teaspoons ground cumin
1½ teaspoons garlic powder
1½ teaspoons dry mustard
1 teaspoon ground ginger

1 teaspoon onion powder
1 teaspoon paprika
1 teaspoon ground dried guajillo
  chile peppers (see pages 1 and 2)
¾ teaspoon cayenne
½ teaspoon black pepper
½ teaspoon white pepper

1½ pounds filet tails
6 tablespoons vegetable oil
½ cup all-purpose flour
1½ cups chopped roasted onions
  (see page4)
¼ cup minced roasted garlic (see
  page 4)
1 cup white potatoes, peeled and
  diced into ½-inch cubes, about 1
  small (7 ounces)

1 cup carrots, peeled and diced
  into ½-inch cubes
1 cup chopped red bell peppers,
  about 1 medium
1 cup chopped yellow bell peppers,
  about 1 medium
4 cups beef stock (see page 6), in all

Combine the seasoning mix ingredients in a small bowl and mix well.

Cut the filet pieces into strips about ¾ inch wide by ¾ inch thick—the length doesn't matter. Working against the grain, cut each strip into ½-inch pieces. Sprinkle the meat evenly with 2 tablespoons of the seasoning mix and rub it in well.

In a heavy 4-quart pot over high heat, heat the oil just until it begins to smoke, about 3 to 4 minutes. Add half the meat and cook, stirring rapidly and constantly to brown the meat on all sides, for 2 minutes. Remove the cooked meat from the pot, set it aside, and repeat the process with the remaining meat.

When the last meat has been removed from the pot, add the flour and mix it with the brown bits remaining in the pot. Cook, whisking constantly, until the mixture turns the color of cinnamon, about 4 minutes. Add the onions, garlic, potatoes, carrots, bell peppers, and ½ cup of the stock. Cook, stirring and scraping the pot constantly, for 2 minutes. Add the remaining seasoning mix and cook, stirring and scraping the pot constantly, for 2 minutes. Add the remaining stock, bring to a boil, reduce the heat to low, and simmer until the vegetables are tender, about 20 to 25 minutes. Return the meat to the pot, increase the heat just until the liquid simmers again, and cook until the meat is just heated through, but still tender, about 6 to 8 minutes. Remove from the heat. Be sure to serve each portion with plenty of the rich gravy—I like to pass the remainder to pour over hot biscuits. Ummmmm!

VEAL
AND
PORK

FROM ALL OVER

Baby Veal Steaks with a Mushroom Melody

MAKES 3 SERVINGS

Shhhh! Listen carefully, and you'll hear how the portobello mushrooms make the veal sing!

SEASONING MIX

1¾ teaspoons paprika
1½ teaspoons ground dried New
  Mexico chile peppers (see pages 1
  and 2)
1½ teaspoons salt
1 teaspoon onion powder
1 teaspoon ground dried Anaheim

chile peppers (see pages 1 and 2)
¾ teaspoon ground ginger
¾ teaspoon dry mustard
½ teaspoon garlic powder
½ teaspoon ground dried árbol chile
  peppers (see pages 1 and 2)
¼ teaspoon ground cumin

6 (10-ounce) baby veal (white veal)
  T-bone steaks
6 tablespoons unsalted butter
1 tablespoon minced fresh ginger
1 teaspoon minced fresh garlic,
  about 1 clove

1 cup thinly sliced green onions,
  about 12 stalks
3 generous tablespoons minced
  fresh basil leaves
2 cups chopped portobello
  mushrooms (see page 169),
  about 1 large (5 ounces)

Combine the seasoning mix ingredients in a small bowl and mix well.

Sprinkle both sides of the steaks evenly with the seasoning mix and rub it in well.

Preheat a 12-inch cast iron skillet over high heat until extremely hot, about 5 to 7 minutes. Place the steaks into the skillet, making sure they have enough room to lay flat, and cook, turning once, until they are browned on both sides and just cooked through, about 2 to 3 minutes per side. Remove the steaks from the skillet as soon as they are cooked and set them aside. Keep them warm while you make the sauce.

Using the same skillet in which the veal steaks were cooked, reduce the heat to low and add the butter. Scrape the bottom of the skillet to loosen all the brown bits and mix them into the butter. Add the ginger, garlic, green onions, and basil. Increase the heat to high and cook, stirring constantly, for 2 minutes. Add the mushrooms and cook, stirring and scraping constantly, until the mushrooms are just cooked, but not too soft, about 2 minutes. Divide the vegetable mixture evenly among the steaks and serve immediately.

Veal Shanks with Okra and Tomato

MAKES 6 SERVINGS

This very delicious veal dish couldn't be easier to cook, yet it's wholesome and satisfying—perfect to prepare for family or guests. In this recipe I tried to have herbs and spices carry the dish, instead of a whole lot of ingredients. Okra and tomatoes work really well together, and in my part of the country are used in many different recipes. By the way, we know bone marrow isn't good for us, but sometimes we just don't care and eat it anyway! I like plenty of hot white rice and buttered corn bread with this.

SEASONING MIX

2 teaspoons salt
1 teaspoon dried chervil leaves
1 teaspoon ground coriander
1 teaspoon garlic powder
1 teaspoon ground ginger
1 teaspoon paprika
1 teaspoon ground dried Anaheim
    chile peppers (see pages 1 and 2)

1 teaspoon ground dried pasilla chile
    peppers (see pages 1 and 2)
1 teaspoon dried thyme leaves
¾ teaspoon cayenne
¾ teaspoon onion powder
½ teaspoon black pepper
¼ teaspoon white pepper

6 (¾-pound) veal shanks, cut for
    osso bucco
¾ pound trimmed and sliced fresh
    okra

2 (15-ounce cans) diced tomatoes
    (see page 7)

Combine the seasoning mix ingredients in a small bowl and mix well.

Sprinkle the veal shanks evenly with 5 teaspoons of the seasoning mix.

Preheat the oven to 350°.

Place the veal shanks in a large roasting pan—no rack is necessary—and roast for 1½ hours.

Remove the shanks from the pan and add the okra, tomatoes, and the remaining seasoning mix. Return the shanks to the pan, turning them over as you do so. Increase the oven temperature to 450° and cook until the shanks are tender, about 1 hour longer. Serve 1 shank per person, surrounded by the cooked vegetables.

Panéed Veal in Cheese Sauce

MAKES 4 SERVINGS

Pané is a south Louisiana term for pan-frying, a popular and traditional cooking method here. Our seasoning mix contains the traditional basil and oregano that you might expect to accompany Italian cheeses, but we've perked it up with a little cayenne, cumin and dill weed. It's very tasty, but a little less peppery than some of my other dishes. If you substitute maple syrup for the cane syrup, be sure to use genuine maple syrup, not flavored pancake syrup. If you're counting calories you can use low-fat sour cream, and substitute puréed low-fat cottage cheese for the heavy cream.

SEASONING MIX

2½ teaspoons salt
2 teaspoons dried basil leaves
1¼ teaspoons garlic powder
1¼ teaspoons onion powder
¾ teaspoon cayenne
¾ teaspoon dry mustard

¾ teaspoon dried oregano leaves
¾ teaspoon paprika
½ teaspoon ground cumin
½ teaspoon dill weed
½ teaspoon black pepper
¼ teaspoon white pepper

8 (3-ounce) baby veal (white veal) cutlets, each 1/8 to ¼ inch thick
2 tablespoons plus 1 teaspoon olive oil, in all
½ cup onions, diced into ¼-inch pieces, about ¼ medium (2 ounces)
½ cup red bell peppers, diced into ¼-inch pieces, about ½ medium
1 zucchini, peeled and diced into ¼-inch pieces
2 teaspoons minced fresh ginger

½ teaspoon minced fresh garlic, about ½ clove
½ cup beef stock (see page 6)
1 cup heavy cream
½ cup sour cream (see page 3)
2 tablespoons cane syrup (see page 165), preferred, or maple syrup
4 ounces freshly grated provolone cheese
4 ounces freshly grated mozzarella cheese

Combine the seasoning mix ingredients in a small bowl and mix well.

If your cutlets are thicker than ¼ inch, pound them between layers of plastic wrap with the flat side of a meat mallet until they're sufficiently flattened. These cutlets are so thin it's easy to over-season them, so be sure to use just the amount of seasoning mix called for. Sprinkle one side of each veal cutlet evenly with ½ teaspoon of the seasoning mix and gently pat it in. Season the other sides of the cutlets by pressing them against the seasoned sides and patting them lightly.

Preheat a heavy 12-inch skillet over high heat until extremely hot, about 8 to 10 minutes. To the skillet add 2 tablespoons of the olive oil and brown the cutlets in the oil, turning quickly, until golden brown on both sides, about 1 to 2 minutes per side. Remove the cutlets to a plate and set them aside.

To the same skillet, add the remaining oil, the onions, and bell peppers. Cook, stirring almost constantly, until the vegetables stick hard, about 3 minutes, then add the zucchini, ginger and garlic. Stir very briefly, then add the stock, the remaining seasoning mix, cream, sour cream, cane (or maple) syrup and cheeses. Whisk until all the cheese is melted, then return the cutlets and the accumulated juices to the skillet, bring just to a boil, and simmer for 1 minute. Serve with your favorite pasta.

Pork Chops in an Onion Gravy

MAKES 6 SERVINGS

The julienne onions in the gravy make these pork chops something to write home about! We've added potato purée to the stock for two reasons: to make the gravy thicker and more flavorful, and to add extra nutrition, as potatoes are a great source of vitamin C. For this dish, I tried to keep the cooking as easy as possible, so it would be quick to prepare.

SEASONING MIX

2½ teaspoons salt
1½ teaspoons onion powder
1 teaspoon dried basil leaves
1 teaspoon ground cardamom
1 teaspoon cayenne
1 teaspoon dried chervil leaves
1 teaspoon ground cumin
1 teaspoon paprika
1 teaspoon ground sage

¾ teaspoon garlic powder
½ teaspoon black pepper
½ teaspoon white pepper
½ teaspoon ground dried árbol chile peppers (see pages 1 and 2)
½ teaspoon ground dried New Mexico chile peppers (see pages 1 and 2)

6 center-cut pork chops, about 1
  inch thick
1½ cups white potatoes, peeled
  and diced into 1-inch cubes,
  about 1 medium-size potato
3 cups pork stock, preferred, or
  chicken stock (see pages 5 and
  6), in all

1 tablespoon vegetable oil
6 cups onions, cut into julienne
  strips (see page 3), about 2 large
  onions
1 tablespoon minced fresh ginger
1 tablespoon minced fresh garlic,
  about 3 cloves
4 tablespoons unsalted butter

Combine the seasoning mix ingredients in a small bowl and mix well.

Sprinkle both sides of the pork chops evenly with 1 tablespoon plus 1 teaspoon of the seasoning mix and rub it in well.

Purée the diced potato with 2 cups of the stock in a blender or food processor and set aside.

In a heavy 12-inch skillet, preferably nonstick, heat the oil just until it begins to smoke, about 3 to 4 minutes. Add the pork chops and cook, turning once, until they are browned on both sides, but not cooked through, about 7 minutes. Remove the pork chops from the skillet and add the onions and 2 teaspoons of the seasoning mix. Cook, stirring the onions about once a minute until they start to brown, about 7 minutes. Remove the onions from the pan and add the ginger, garlic, butter, potato purée, the remaining stock, and the remaining seasoning mix. Whisk the mixture until it returns to a full boil, then lower the heat to medium and simmer briskly for 6 minutes. Return the pork chops and the accumulated juices to the skillet along with the onions. Simmer until the pork chops are cooked through and tender, but not overcooked. After the chops have simmered for 15 minutes, check them for doneness by cutting into the thickest part. If it's white, they're done. If the meat is still pink, they're not done, so continue to simmer, checking again at 5 and 10 minutes. Do not let them simmer for more than 25 minutes in all. Be sure each portion has plenty of the wonderful onion gravy!

Roasted Pork Tenderloin with Rosemary Potatoes

Photograph No. 7

MAKES 6 GENEROUS SERVINGS

The pan drippings are important in this dish—get them all and you will be getting the finest flavor of the roast! The fresh rosemary also is essential, to the roast as well as to the potatoes, so don't substitute. Even if you don't have an herb garden, more and more supermarkets all over the country carry fresh herbs these days, so you shouldn't have a problem finding it. If you don't see it, ask the produce manager to order it for you, or seek out small, specialty grocers, where shopping can be as much fun and adventurous as cooking, and you're likely to meet some wonderfully interesting people!

SEASONING MIX

2 teaspoons salt
1½ teaspoons ground cumin
1½ teaspoons dry mustard
1½ teaspoons dried thyme leaves
1 teaspoon ground allspice

1 teaspoon garlic powder
1 teaspoon onion powder
1 teaspoon paprika
¾ teaspoon cayenne
½ teaspoon black pepper

STUFFING

1 tablespoon vegetable oil
1 cup chopped onions, about 1
  small (5 ounces)
1 cup chopped celery, about 2
  stalks
½ cup chopped red bell peppers,
  about ½ medium

¾ cup chopped yellow bell
  peppers, about ¾ medium
1 tablespoon minced fresh ginger
1 teaspoon minced fresh garlic,
  about 3 cloves
½ cup pork stock, preferred, or
  chicken stock (see pages 5 and 6)

3 large white potatoes
3 large sweet potatoes
2 quarts plus 2½ cups pork stock,
  preferred, or chicken stock (see
  pages 5 and 6), in all
2 teaspoons salt

1 tablespoon plus 1½ teaspoons olive
  oil
1 tablespoon chopped fresh
  rosemary, in all
1 (1½- to 2-pound) pork tenderloin
½ cup sour cream (see page 3)

Combine the seasoning mix ingredients in a small bowl and mix well.

STUFFING In a heavy 12-inch skillet over high heat, heat the oil just until it begins to smoke, about 3 to 4 minutes. Add the onions, celery, bell peppers, ginger, garlic, and 2 tablespoons of the seasoning mix. Cook, stirring every 2 or 3 minutes, until the vegetables are well browned, about 20 minutes. Add the stock, then scrape the skillet bottom thoroughly, dissolving the brown bits. Remove from the heat and set aside.

ROSEMARY POTATOES Do not peel the potatoes, but scrub them and cut them in half lengthwise.

In a 6-quart pot over high heat, bring 2 quarts of the stock to a boil and add all the potato halves. Boil for 12 minutes, then remove the white potatoes. Boil the sweet potato halves for 5 minutes more, then remove and season all the potatoes with the salt, reserving the stock. When the potatoes are cool, rub them with the olive oil, then sprinkle all the cut sides evenly with a total of 2 teaspoons of the rosemary.

TENDERLOIN Preheat the oven to 450°.

Make a series of pockets for the stuffing: insert a knife through the top of the meat, then push the knife almost all the way through, and, without enlarging the opening, move the knife back and forth to form a pocket. Repeat this process, making rows of pockets about ¾ of an inch apart. Spoon the stuffing into the pockets and force it down with the back of a spoon or by pushing it down with your fingers. Sprinkle the remaining rosemary over the tenderloin. Set aside.

Place the potatoes in a roasting pan and roast for 10 minutes. Lower the oven temperature to 250°, place the tenderloin in the pan and cook until the meat's internal temperature (determined by inserting a meat thermometer about halfway into the roast), reaches the temperature for the degree of doneness you prefer:

> *Well done* *160° about 1 hour and 40 minutes*
> *Medium* *140°*

Remove and peel one sweet potato half and one white potato half. Drain off and reserve the pan drippings. Keep the roast and remaining potato halves warm while you make the sauce.

SAUCE In a medium saucepan over high heat, combine the remaining 2½ cups of stock, the peeled potato halves, the reserved pan drippings, and the remaining seasoning mix. Bring just to a boil, then remove from the heat and purée. Return the purée to high heat, bring to a boil, then whisk in the sour cream and as much of the reserved stock (in which the potatoes were cooked) as needed to make the sauce as thick as you like it. Return just to a boil, remove from the heat, and whisk until the sour cream is completely distributed.

To serve, slice the roast, add a potato half to each portion, and drizzle with some of the sauce. Pass the remaining sauce separately.

Banana Pepper Casserole

MAKES 6 TO 8 SERVINGS

On the television show, this recipe was done as individual stuffed peppers. This is very similar to the original version, which we all thought was delicious, but after the taping I decided to try something different, and what follows is the result. You know what? It's even better!

I like to come up with unusual taste combinations, and think I hit the jackpot here. You might never expect rutabagas to go with these peppers, but they do! This is an easy recipe to prepare—it looks lengthy only because we've explained everything carefully. There are also a couple of notes within the recipe, right where you'll need them, so be on the lookout for this special information. As you read the ingredients list, you'll notice that ground dried Anaheim chile peppers are listed twice, once in the seasoning mix, and once in the sauce. This is correct; first you mix up the main seasonings, then you combine 6 tablespoons of that mixture with the additional 2 tablespoons Anaheims (or paprika if you prefer less heat) for the sauce. Use masa harina or corn flour if you have it, but you don't have to buy it just for this recipe—it tastes great and goes well with the enchilada-type sauce, but you can use all-purpose flour.

I like to serve this casserole with more tortillas, either cut into strips or rolled up. Or serve them in a covered, heated dish and let your guests butter and roll them themselves, the way they do in Tex-Mex restaurants.

2 tablespoons salt
1 tablespoon plus 1 teaspoon dried
   basil leaves
1 tablespoon plus 1 teaspoon paprika
1 tablespoon plus 1 teaspoon ground
   dried Anaheim chile peppers (see
   pages 1 and 2)
1 tablespoon ground cumin

1 tablespoon ground ginger
1 tablespoon onion powder
2 teaspoons dry mustard
2 teaspoons black pepper
1 teaspoon cayenne
1 teaspoon garlic powder
1 teaspoon white pepper

SAUCE

2 tablespoons ground dried
   Anaheim chile peppers (see
   pages 1 and 2) or paprika
¼ cup vegetable oil
About ½ cup all-purpose flour
1 cup chopped onions, about 1
   small (5 ounces)

2 medium-size red bell peppers,
   roasted (see page 4), and
   chopped
3½ cups chicken stock (see pages 5
   and 6), in all
1 tablespoon dark brown sugar, if
   necessary or desired

4 banana peppers (see page 165),
   cut in half lengthwise, ribs,
   seeds and stems removed

Vegetable oil for frying
12 (6-inch diameter) corn tortillas

MEAT AND VEGETABLE MIXTURE

2 tablespoons olive oil
2 cups onions, diced into ¼-inch
   cubes, about 1 medium (10
   ounces)
1 cup banana peppers (see page
   165), diced into ¼-inch cubes
1 cup red bell peppers, diced into
   ¼-inch cubes, about 1 medium
1 cup yellow bell peppers, diced
   into ¼-inch cubes, about 1
   medium
2 teaspoons minced fresh ginger
½ cup celery, diced into ¼-inch
   cubes, about 1 stalk

1 medium-size rutabaga (see page
   171), about 1½ pounds, peeled
   and diced into ¼-inch cubes,
   about 3 cups
1½ cups pork stock, preferred, or
   vegetable stock or chicken stock
   (see pages 5 and 6), in all
¼ cup masa harina (see page 169),
   or corn flour, or all-purpose flour
½ pound ground pork
1½ cups pork stock, preferred, or
   vegetable stock or chicken stock
   (see pages 5 and 6)

4 (8-inch) flour tortillas, in all
10 ounces freshly grated Monterey
   Jack cheese, in all

1 cup sour cream (see page 3)

Combine the seasoning mix ingredients in a small bowl (but not too small—because the mixture will be almost 12 tablespoons—a coffee mug or cereal bowl will be the right size) and mix well.

SAUCE Combine 6 tablespoons of the seasoning mix with the 2 tablespoons Anaheim chile peppers (or paprika) listed in the sauce ingredients in a small bowl and mix well.

In a 12-inch skillet or a heavy 2-quart saucepan over high heat, heat the oil just until it begins to smoke, about 6 minutes. Add the flour, a little at a time, and cook, whisking constantly, until the flour is nut-brown. *The exact amount of flour you need will vary according to the kind of flour and how much moisture is naturally in it; usually we use equal parts oil and flour, but not always. The consistency you're looking for is smooth and not liquid, but still flowing. This is one time when you have to follow your eyes and mind, not the measuring cup or clock.* Keep whisking the roux thoroughly and cook until it becomes a dark reddish-brown, which will take anywhere from 2 to 5 minutes from the time you first add the flour—but watch the roux, not the clock! As soon as the roux reaches the right color, immediately add the onions and bell peppers, and turn off the heat. Whisk for 1 minute then whisk in the Anaheim peppers/seasoning mix and 1 cup of the stock. Turn the heat back on, whisk well, and when the mixture is thoroughly blended stir in 1 cup stock. Cook and whisk for 1 more minute, then whisk in the remaining stock. Cook, whisking every 2 minutes, for 8 minutes, then, if desired, add the brown sugar. *Sometimes roasted Anaheim peppers or paprika will be bitter, but we want their great basic flavor, so taste the sauce, and if it seems bitter to you, add the sugar. Or add it if you think you'd like it better that way!* Reduce the heat to medium and simmer briskly, stirring every 2 to 3 minutes, until the sauce is rich and thick, about 15 to 17 minutes, then remove from the heat. It will be a gorgeous dark reddish-brown color and incredibly fragrant. Taste the sauce again, and if you would like the bell pepper taste to be a little sweeter, or if you prefer a smoother sauce, purée the mixture in a food processor or blender and set it aside.

PEPPERS Parboil the 8 banana pepper halves in briskly boiling water for 5 minutes, then drain and set them aside.

TORTILLA CRUMBS Pour enough vegetable oil into a 10-inch skillet to measure 1 inch deep and place over high heat until the oil begins to smoke, about 6 to 7 minutes. Fry all the corn tortillas, one at a time, turning once or twice, until they are golden brown and crispy. When the oil stops bubbling, the moisture has evaporated from the tortillas—a sure sign they are done. Drain the tortillas on paper towels, and when they are cool enough to handle, break them into pieces and pulverize them in a food processor. Or you can pulverize the tortillas by placing them in a strong plastic bag (don't seal it, or the trapped air will keep you from being able to apply pressure) and crushing them with a rolling pin. Set aside.

MEAT AND VEGETABLE MIXTURE In a heavy 12-inch nonstick skillet over high heat, heat the olive oil just until it begins to smoke, about 3 to 4 minutes. Add the onions, diced banana peppers, all the bell peppers, the ginger and celery. Stir, cover the skillet, and cook for 5 minutes, then uncover and stir thoroughly. Continue to cook, uncovered, stirring every 2 minutes, for 6 minutes, then stir in the rutabaga and cook for 2 minutes. Stir in ½ cup stock, re-cover, and cook for 4 minutes. Uncover and stir—you'll see that the vegetables are just barely beginning to brown because of all their liquid, so re-cover and continue cooking for 2 minutes. Uncover and stir again—you'll notice that almost all of the liquid has evaporated and the rutabaga is still a little crunchy but getting tender. Now add the masa harina and the remaining seasoning mix (the reason we didn't add the seasoning mix in stages, as I usually do, is that we're cooking it here in the skillet and will cook it again in the oven, which is similar to the multiple-cooking of adding it in stages.) By now you should be able to smell and taste the "roasting corn" of the masa harina, even though it's slightly moistened by the vegetables, because it's really getting hot. Continue to cook, stirring every 2 minutes, for 6 minutes, then stir in the ground pork. We can add the meat late in the cooking because it will be thoroughly cooked in the oven—we're just getting it started now. Break up the clumps of meat as you stir it into the other ingredients. You will notice that the herbs and spices are getting really dark now—almost black—but that's OK, because toasting them like this really brings out their flavor. After the meat is thoroughly mixed in, mash down and spread the mixture on the bottom of the skillet so it will brown well. Cook undisturbed for 2 minutes, then stir, mash and cook for 2 minutes, and again stir, mash and cook for 2 minutes longer. After the third stirring, mashing and cooking, stir in the remaining cup of stock, and as soon as it's mixed in well remove from the heat.

Preheat the oven to 350°.

In a 9-inch by 13-inch casserole dish or baking pan, layer the components of the casserole in the following order: first, half the sauce, or a little more than 1½ cups. Next, place 2 of the whole tortillas, then

4 of the roasted banana pepper halves. Now gently but evenly spread half the meat and vegetable mixture over the layers in the dish, and then sprinkle half the grated cheese evenly over the meat and vegetable mixture. Repeat the layers: remaining sauce, whole tortillas, pepper halves, meat and vegetable mixture, and *now the sour cream*, then the remaining grated cheese. Bake until the casserole is bubbly and the cheese is nicely browned, about 40 to 45 minutes. A good way to tell if it's perfectly done is to check the internal temperature with a meat thermometer—it should be 160°.

Just before serving, sprinkle the tortilla crumbs evenly on top of the casserole, or if you're serving buffet style, offer the crumbs in a separate dish and let everyone help himself.

Stuffed Portobello Caps

MAKES 8 APPETIZER SERVINGS

This is a very special dish, impressive as an appetizer or as a side dish with a roast. Some markets sell mushroom caps, with the stems already removed. Portobello mushrooms are simply white mushrooms that have been hybridized so they will grow very large—their caps can measure up to 6 inches in diameter.

SEASONING MIX

2 teaspoons paprika
1½ teaspoons salt
1 teaspoon ground coriander
1 teaspoon garlic powder
1 teaspoon onion powder
1 teaspoon dried thyme leaves
¾ teaspoon cayenne

¾ teaspoon ground cinnamon
½ teaspoon ground allspice
½ teaspoon black pepper
½ teaspoon white pepper
½ teaspoon ground dried árbol chile peppers (see pages 1 and 2)

1 medium-size eggplant
2 tablespoons unseasoned bread crumbs
2 tablespoons vegetable oil
1½ cups minced onions, about 1 medium

1 cup minced celery, about 2 stalks
1 cup minced red bell peppers, about 1 medium
1 cup minced yellow bell peppers, about 1 medium

6 ounces andouille (see page 165) or your favorite smoked pork sausage, quartered lengthwise, then cut into ¼-inch pieces

2 cups portobello mushrooms (see page 169), diced into ¼-inch pieces, about 1 large (5 ounces)

1 cup vegetable stock (see pages 5 and 6)

8 teaspoons cane syrup (see page 165), preferred, or pure maple syrup

8 (5-inch diameter) portobello mushrooms (see page 169)

Preheat the oven to 450°.

Pierce the eggplant 8 or 10 times with a skewer or fork, then roast in the oven, on an upper rack (with foil or a baking sheet on the rack below to catch any drippings), until the skin is soft, brown, and pulls away from the pulp, about 25 to 30 minutes. It will look puffy and will wrinkle easily when touched. When the eggplant is cool enough to handle, cut it in half lengthwise and scrape out the pulp. Discard the peel and set the pulp aside.

In a small skillet over high heat, toast the bread crumbs, stirring constantly to prevent burning, until they begin to brown, about 3 to 4 minutes. Remove the crumbs from the skillet to stop the toasting and set them aside.

Combine the seasoning mix ingredients in a small bowl and mix well.

In a 12-inch cast-iron skillet over high heat, heat the oil just until it begins to smoke, about 3 to 4 minutes. Add the onions, celery, bell peppers, eggplant, andouille, and seasoning mix. Cover and cook, uncovering every 3 to 4 minutes to stir and mash the eggplant, breaking up and distributing the pulp, until the vegetables wilt and begin to brown, about 18 minutes. Add the diced mushrooms and cook, uncovered, stirring and scraping every 1 or 2 minutes, for 10 minutes. Stir in the stock and cook for 10 minutes more. Remove from the heat and cool.

Preheat the oven to 350°.

Prepare the mushrooms for stuffing by removing the stems at the bases, where they meet the "gills" (see page 167). Place the mushroom caps, stem sides up, in a baking pan, and drizzle 1 teaspoon syrup over the inside of each mushroom cap. Mound 6 tablespoons of the stuffing into each cap and top with 1 teaspoon of the bread crumbs. Bake until the mushroom caps are tender and the crumb topping just begins to brown, about 15 minutes. Serve hot.

WINGED WONDERS

OF THE WORLD

San Antonio Chicken

MAKES 4 SERVINGS

This beautiful dish is peppery, as you might guess, but not too hot for most people. It gets its name from the combination of chicken, onions, bell peppers, and corn tortillas found in Tex-Mex recipes. If you can't find ground sage, you can use rubbed. To turn the evening into a fiesta, start with cool drinks and tortilla chips with Pico de Gallo (page 44), and a salad of guacamole on thinly sliced tomatoes. An appropriate dessert might be lemon ice cream (not sherbet) with sugar cookies or pecan/nougat roll candy. Si, si, señor!

SEASONING MIX

1¾ teaspoons dried oregano leaves
1¾ teaspoons salt
1½ teaspoons ground cumin
1½ teaspoons onion powder
1¼ teaspoons paprika
¾ teaspoon garlic powder
¾ teaspoon ground dried guajillo chile peppers (see pages 1 and 2)

¾ teaspoon ground dried New Mexico chile peppers (see pages 1 and 2)
¾ teaspoon ground sage
½ teaspoon black pepper
¼ teaspoon cayenne
¼ teaspoon white pepper

¼ cup all-purpose flour
¼ cup ground dried Anaheim chile peppers (see pages 1 and 2)
1 (4-pound) chicken, cut into 8 pieces
2 cups chopped onions, about 1 large (10 ounces)
1 cup chopped celery, about 2 stalks
1½ cups chopped green bell peppers, about 1½ medium

1½ cups chopped red bell peppers, about 1½ medium
1½ cups chopped yellow bell peppers, about 1½ medium
3½ cups chicken stock (see pages 5 and 6), in all
½ teaspoon minced fresh garlic, about ½ clove
4 (6-inch) corn tortillas, cut into julienne strips (see page 3), about 3 or 4 inches long, and as narrow as possible

Combine the seasoning mix ingredients in a small bowl and mix well.

In a small skillet over high heat, brown the flour, stirring and shaking constantly, until it is the color of light milk chocolate. Immediately remove the flour from the skillet to stop the browning and whisk in the ground Anaheim chile peppers until they are fully blended and have the rich aroma of roasted peppers.

Sprinkle the chicken evenly with 1 tablespoon plus 2 teaspoons of the seasoning mix and rub it in well.

Preheat a heavy 4-quart pot over high heat for 4 minutes. Add the chicken in batches, large pieces first and skin sides down first, and cook, turning frequently, until golden brown but not fully cooked. Remove the chicken from the pot and set it aside. To the pot add the onions, celery, bell peppers, and the remaining seasoning mix. Cook, stirring and scraping up all the browned bits on the pan bottom every 4 or 5 minutes, for 15 minutes. If during this time the brown bits begin to stick hard and you feel it's necessary to deglaze (a culinary term meaning to use a liquid to loosen and dissolve the stuck bits) the pot, add ½ cup stock (no more, though, because too much stock will keep the vegetables from browning) and use it to dissolve the bits. At the end of the 15 minutes, add ½ cup stock and scrape the sides and bottom of the pot. Add the browned flour/chile peppers mixture and the garlic, and stir until the flour is absorbed and the mixture forms a brown-red paste. Stir in the remaining stock, scrape the pan well, then switch to a whisk and agitate the liquid until the paste is absorbed—don't let it settle. There is a chance the flour might burn if it is allowed to settle on the bottom of the pot, so avoid the possibility by constant whisking. The sauce should now be a rich red-brown. Bring it to a boil, then return the chicken and the accumulated juices to the pot, along with the tortilla strips. Return just to a boil, then reduce the heat to low, cover and simmer, uncovering to stir every 5 minutes, until the chicken is done, about 15 minutes. Serve hot.

Opelousas "Double O" Chicken

MAKES 4 SERVINGS

This dish got its name when I was taping the television series of recipes from this book because I'm from Opelousas, Louisiana's third oldest city, and so is Marty Cosgrove, the executive chef at Magic Seasoning Blends, who assisted with food preparation for the show. Not only is this dish quick and simple to prepare, it's low in calories. The combination of cabbage and sweet potatoes is unusual, but works extremely well, giving the chicken a whole new flavor direction, and I think the colors look good together too. It's great served over pasta, rice, or even mashed potatoes.

SEASONING MIX

2 teaspoons salt
1½ teaspoons dry mustard
1½ teaspoons paprika
1 teaspoon cayenne
1 teaspoon ground dried Anaheim
    chile peppers (see pages 1 and 2)

1 teaspoon ground dried guajillo
    chile peppers (see pages 1 and 2)
¾ teaspoon ground cumin
¾ teaspoon garlic powder
¾ teaspoon onion powder
½ teaspoon black pepper

8 boneless, skinless chicken breast
    halves, each about 4 ounces
½ cup chopped onions, about ½
    small (3 ounces)
3 cups sweet potatoes, diced into
    ½-inch cubes, about 1
    medium-large (1 pound), in all

2½ cups green cabbage, diced into
    1-inch cubes, about ¼ medium
    head, in all
4 cups chicken stock (see pages 5
    and 6) in all

Combine the seasoning mix ingredients in a small bowl and mix well.

Sprinkle the chicken evenly with 1 tablespoon plus 1 teaspoon of the seasoning mix and gently pat it in.

Preheat a heavy 4-quart pot over high heat until it is very hot, about 4 minutes. Add the chicken, in batches if necessary, and cook, turning frequently, just until it begins to brown (it will not be fully cooked at this time), about 4 minutes per batch. Remove the chicken and set it aside.

To the pot add the onions, ½ cup of the sweet potatoes, and 1½ cups of the cabbage. Let the vegetables sit in the pot for about 1 minute —they will release some moisture. Scrape the bottom of the pot thoroughly, using the moisture to help loosen the brown bits from the bottom of the pot. If the vegetables do not produce enough liquid to dissolve all the brown bits, add ½ cup stock. Cook, stirring and scraping every 2 minutes, for 8 minutes, then stir in 1 cup of the stock and the remaining seasoning mix. Cover the pot and continue to cook, uncovering to scrape the bottom of the pot every 3 or 4 minutes, until the mixture has thickened, about 10 minutes. Add the remaining vegetables and the remaining stock. Stir and scrape the pot bottom, then re-cover and cook for 15 minutes. Uncover and return the chicken breasts and the accumulated juices to the pot, reduce the heat to medium, re-cover and simmer briskly until the breasts are cooked through, about 10 to 13 minutes. Serve piping hot.

Chicken Breasts with Cilantro

MAKES 4 SERVINGS

If you are unable to find ground fenugreek, don't worry—the seeds are more readily available, and it's easy to grind them yourself. We've found a small, inexpensive coffee grinder works great to grind spices, and those that are freshly ground are likely to be more pungent anyway. The fresh cilantro is very important to the flavor of this dish, so don't substitute anything else. Just because cilantro looks very much like flat parsley doesn't mean the taste is the same!

SEASONING MIX

2 teaspoons salt
1 teaspoon garlic powder
1 teaspoon onion powder
1 teaspoon turmeric
¾ teaspoon ground cardamom
¾ teaspoon cayenne
¾ teaspoon ground cumin

¾ teaspoon ground fenugreek (see page 167)
¾ teaspoon black pepper
½ teaspoon ground allspice
½ teaspoon ground ginger
½ teaspoon ground dried pasilla chile peppers (see pages 1 and 2)

8 chicken breast halves, about 1½ to 2 pounds total
2 tablespoons olive oil
1 cup chopped onions, about 1 small (5 ounces)
½ cup chopped green bell peppers, about ½ medium
½ cup chopped red bell peppers, about ½ medium
½ cup chopped yellow bell peppers, about ½ medium
¾ cup chopped celery, about 1 large or 2 small stalks
2 tablespoons minced fresh serrano chile peppers (see pages 1 and 2), optional

1 tablespoon minced fresh ginger
1 teaspoon minced fresh garlic, about 1 clove
2½ cups chicken stock (see pages 5 and 6), in all
3 tablespoons all-purpose flour
3½ cups unpeeled zucchini, diced into ½-inch pieces
1 (15-ounce) can diced tomatoes (see page 7)
1 pound short pasta (rotini, fuselli or gemelli), cooked and drained, about 5 cups
1½ cups lightly packed fresh cilantro leaves, stems removed

Combine the seasoning mix ingredients in a small bowl and mix well.

Sprinkle the chicken evenly with 1 tablespoon plus 2 teaspoons of the seasoning mix and rub it in well.

Preheat a heavy 12-inch skillet over high heat until very hot, about 6 to 8 minutes. Add the oil, then add the chicken breasts. Cook, in batches if necessary, turning once, until browned on both sides, but not fully cooked through, about 7 minutes per batch. Remove the chicken from the skillet and set it aside.

To the same skillet add the onions, bell peppers, celery, serrano chile peppers, ginger, garlic, and 2 tablespoons of the seasoning mix. Cook, stirring and scraping the pot every 1 or 2 minutes, until the mixture begins to stick, about 5 minutes. Stir in ½ cup stock and cook, stirring and scraping the skillet every 2 minutes, until the stock is almost evaporated, about 10 minutes. Stir in another ½ cup of stock and scrape the pot thoroughly. Add the flour and stir until it is completely absorbed. Add the zucchini and the remaining seasoning mix and cook, stirring and scraping every 1 or 2 minutes, until the mixture is reduced in volume and a crust forms on the bottom, about 5 to 6 minutes. Add the tomatoes, scrape well, stir in the remaining stock, cover, and cook for 10 minutes. Uncover and stir well, add the cooked pasta and the cilantro and stir well again. Return the chicken and the accumulated juices to the pot, re-cover, and cook until the pasta is warmed through, about 5 minutes. Remove from the heat and serve immediately. Make sure that each serving includes a generous portion of the pasta and sauce.

Chicken in Leek Sauce

MAKES 4 SERVINGS

Leeks, related to garlic and onions, look like giant scallions. In earlier days they were thought to have hidden powers, such as making you stronger and giving you a beautiful singing voice. And in the Dark Ages, the Welsh used them as their national symbol, believing they helped them vanquish their enemies. I don't know about improving your voice or beating your enemies, but I do know they add a great flavor and texture to soups and sauces. The smaller the leek, the more tender it will be. If you can't find ground sage, you can use rubbed. Notice that this dish is cooked entirely without oil, so when you're browning the chicken you need to be careful that it doesn't burn. If your stove is a dragon, lower the heat, and use the heaviest pot you have.

SEASONING MIX

1¼ teaspoons paprika
1¼ teaspoons salt
¾ teaspoon ground ginger
¾ teaspoon onion powder
½ teaspoon ground dried Anaheim
    chile peppers (see pages 1 and 2)
½ teaspoon ground sage

½ teaspoon cayenne
½ teaspoon ground cumin
½ teaspoon garlic powder
½ teaspoon black pepper
½ teaspoon ground savory
¼ teaspoon white pepper

1 (3½- to 4-pound) chicken, cut
    into 8 pieces
1½ cups leeks, white portion only,
    cut into ¼-inch julienne strips
    (see page 3), in all
½ cup red bell peppers, cut into
    ¼-inch julienne strips (see page
    3)

½ cup yellow bell peppers, cut into
    ¼-inch julienne strips (see page
    3)
2¼ cups chicken stock (see pages 5
    and 6), in all
2 tablespoons all-purpose flour
4 cups bok choy leaves (stems
    discarded), torn into pieces

Combine the seasoning mix ingredients in a small bowl and mix well.

Sprinkle the chicken evenly with 1 tablespoon plus 1 teaspoon of the seasoning mix and rub it in well.

Preheat a heavy 4-quart pot over high heat until very hot, about 3 to 4 minutes. Add the chicken, in batches if necessary, large pieces first and skin sides down first, and cook, turning several times, until brown on both sides but not fully cooked. If the second batch of chicken does not fill up the pot, add some of the leeks and let them sit in the empty spot without stirring—their moisture will help prevent burning. Remove the chicken pieces from the pot as they brown.

When all the chicken is removed, add 1 cup of the leeks and all the bell peppers to the pot. Scrape the bottom of the pot, then add the remaining seasoning mix. Cook, stirring every minute at first then almost constantly, until the mixture begins to stick hard and the vegetables start to brown, about 5 minutes. Add ½ cup of stock and scrape the bottom and the sides of the pot. Bring to a boil, then add the flour, working it into the mixture until it is completely absorbed. Add the remaining leeks and the bok choy. Cook without stirring until a crust forms, about 4 minutes. When the crust is red-brown, stir in the remaining stock and scrape the pot thoroughly until all the brown bits are dissolved. Return the chicken and the accumulated juices to the pot, bring to a boil, then reduce heat to low and simmer until the chicken is cooked through, about 12 minutes. Serve hot.

Chicken in Butternut Squash

MAKES 4 TO 6 SERVINGS

This attractive dish is packed with nutrients, but what excites me about it is the great taste. The sweet spices bring out the sunshine in squash, and the fresh garlic pushes up the other flavors—you don't taste it, but it tames acid or hot flavors. Plantains, popular all over the tropics, have a lot of starch and a tendency to sweetness, which also controls any bitterness and the heat from the peppers. If butternut squash is unavailable when you shop, you can substitute acorn or any firm, golden-fleshed squash.

SEASONING MIX

2½ teaspoons salt
1½ teaspoons onion powder
1 teaspoon garlic powder
1 teaspoon paprika
1 teaspoon ground sage
¾ teaspoon cayenne
¾ teaspoon ground savory

¾ teaspoon dried thyme leaves
½ teaspoon ground cinnamon
½ teaspoon ground nutmeg
½ teaspoon dry mustard
½ teaspoon black pepper
¼ teaspoon white pepper

1 (3- to 4-pound) chicken, cut into
   8 pieces
1 medium-size butternut squash,
   about 2½ to 3 pounds, diced into
   ½-inch pieces, about 6 cups, in
   all
2 cups chopped onions, about 1
   medium-large (10 ounces)
1 cup chopped yellow bell peppers,
   about 1 medium

1 cup ripe plantain, diced into
   ½-inch cubes, about 1 medium
   (8 ounces)
1 tablespoon minced fresh ginger
2 teaspoons minced fresh garlic,
   about 2 cloves
3½ cups chicken stock (see pages 5
   and 6), in all

Combine the seasoning mix ingredients in a small bowl and mix well.

Sprinkle the chicken evenly with 1 tablespoon plus 1 teaspoon of the seasoning mix and rub it in well.

Preheat a heavy 4-quart pot over high heat until it is very hot, about 4 minutes. Add the chicken, in batches if necessary, large pieces first and skin sides down first, and cook, turning frequently, until golden brown but not fully cooked, about 8 minutes per batch. Remove the chicken and set it aside, leaving in the pot as much of the seasoning mix and chicken fat as possible.

To the same pot, add 3 cups of the squash, the onions, bell peppers, plantain, ginger, garlic, and the remaining seasoning mix. Stir well, add 1 cup stock and scrape up all the browned bits on the pot bottom. Cook, stirring and scraping every 2 or 3 minutes, until a golden brown crust forms and sticks hard to the pot, about 15 minutes. Stir in 1 cup of the stock, then scrape the pot bottom thoroughly. Cook until the starches from the squash and plantain begin to thicken the mixture, about 6 to 8 minutes. Stir in the remaining stock, then switch to a whisk and use it to break up the plantain and squash to help thicken the sauce. Add the remaining squash, return the chicken and the accumulated juices to the pot, and bring to a boil. Reduce the heat to low and simmer until the chicken is cooked through, about 12 minutes. Serve hot—it's especially good with brown rice.

Chicken Breasts with Smoked Gouda

MAKES 4 SERVINGS

This chicken is not only great tasting, but it's really a fine-looking dish. Each serving consists of two individual chicken breasts topped with slices of the cheese, which melt somewhat but still hold their shape, served with a creamy sauce spiked with green onions and well-balanced seasonings. Picture perfect!

Because the flavor of the Gouda cheese is dominant in this recipe, the kind you use is extremely important. Try to find a variety with the outside smoky rind still on it, and be sure it is not coated with wax. The best choice is Hollandia®, with Bruder Basil® as an alternative. If you are not using a nonstick skillet, you may want to use 2 tablespoons of vegetable oil to coat the skillet before you brown the chicken. Of course if you are using nonstick cookware you'll need to use a plastic whisk.

SEASONING MIX

1¾ teaspoons salt
¾ teaspoon dried basil leaves
¾ teaspoon cayenne
¾ teaspoon ground cumin
¾ teaspoon ground ginger
¾ teaspoon onion powder
¾ teaspoon dried oregano leaves

¾ teaspoon paprika
½ teaspoon ground dried árbol chile
   peppers (see pages 1 and 2)
½ teaspoon garlic powder
½ teaspoon black pepper
½ teaspoon ground savory
¼ teaspoon white pepper

8 (4-ounce) boneless, skinless
    chicken breast halves
1 pound smoked Gouda cheese
1 tablespoon plus 1½ teaspoons
    minced fresh ginger
1 tablespoon plus 1½ teaspoons
    minced fresh garlic, about 4 to 5
    cloves

¾ cup thinly sliced green onions,
    about 8 stalks
3 tablespoons unsalted butter (or
    more if necessary)
3 tablespoons all-purpose flour
2 cups chicken stock (see pages 5
    and 6)
1½ cups sour cream (see page 3)
¾ cup yogurt (see page 3)

Combine the seasoning mix ingredients in a small bowl and mix well.

Sprinkle the breast halves evenly with 1 tablespoon plus 1 teaspoon
of the seasoning mix and gently rub it in. Set aside.

Slice off the smoky rind of the Gouda cheese and dice it finely. Cut 16
thin slices from the cheese and finely dice the remainder—you should
have about ½ cup.

Heat a 12-inch nonstick skillet until it is very hot, about 4 minutes.
Add 4 of the seasoned breast halves and cook until they are brown on
one side, about 3 minutes. Turn them over and place 2 slices of the
cheese on top of each breast. Cook until the underside is browned—the
chicken will not be cooked through at this point. Carefully remove the
breasts from the skillet and set aside.

To the same skillet add the ginger, garlic, green onions, remaining
seasoning mix, and butter and push them all to one side. Cook the
remaining chicken breasts in the same way as the first batch. Remove
the cheese-topped chicken and stir in the flour. Mix it in well until it
is absorbed, and if there is not enough moisture to absorb all the flour,
add a little more butter. Whisk in the stock thoroughly, then whisk
in the sour cream and yogurt. Add the diced Gouda rind and cheese.
Bring just to a boil, reduce the heat to low, and carefully return the
cheese-topped chicken breasts to the skillet. Simmer until the chicken
is cooked through, occasionally spooning some of the sauce over the
top of the chicken to melt the cheese, about 5 minutes. Serve two
breast halves per person, over pasta or rice, and be sure everyone gets
plenty of the wonderful sauce.

Pepper Jack Chicken

MAKES 4 TO 6 SERVINGS

I know you can buy Pepper Jack cheese, but by using a good quality Monterey Jack cheese plus fresh chile peppers in this recipe, you're going to get a much fresher, sharper flavor. The apples are sort of a secret ingredient, giving the dish a bit of mystery—anyone tasting it without knowing might not be able to guess, especially if you've done a thorough job of mashing.

SEASONING MIX

1½ teaspoons dried basil leaves
1½ teaspoons ground coriander
1½ teaspoons ground cumin
1½ teaspoons ground ginger
1½ teaspoons onion powder
1½ teaspoons ground sage

1 teaspoon salt
¾ teaspoon garlic powder
½ teaspoon black pepper
¼ teaspoon cayenne
¼ teaspoon white pepper

1 (3- to 4-pound) chicken, cut into 8 pieces
2 tablespoons vegetable oil
1 cup chopped onions, about 1 small (5 ounces)
1 cup bok choy stems, diced into ¼-inch pieces
1 thinly sliced fresh serrano chile pepper (see pages 1 and 2)
1 thinly sliced fresh bird's eye or Thai chile pepper (see pages 1 and 2)
2 tablespoons minced jalapeño chile peppers (see pages 1 and 2)

1½ teaspoons minced fresh garlic, about 1½ cloves
1 teaspoon minced fresh ginger
1 tablespoon all-purpose flour
1½ cups chicken stock (see pages 5 and 6), in all
6 ounces freshly grated Monterey Jack cheese
1¼ cups unpeeled Gala or McIntosh apples, cored and chopped
¼ cup heavy cream

Combine the seasoning mix ingredients in a small bowl and mix well.

Sprinkle the chicken evenly with 1 tablespoon plus 1 teaspoon of the seasoning mix and rub it in well.

Heat the oil in a heavy 4-quart pot over high heat just until it begins to smoke, about 3 to 4 minutes. Add the chicken in batches, large pieces first and skin sides down first, and cook, turning about once a minute, until golden brown but not fully cooked, about 8 minutes per batch. Remove the chicken from the pot and set it aside.

To the same pot add the onions, bok choy, chile peppers, garlic, ginger, and the remaining seasoning mix. Cook, stirring and scraping up the brown bits once a minute, for 5 minutes (this is very dry without any bell peppers, so you may need to reduce the heat a little), then add the flour. Stir and mash the mixture constantly until the flour is absorbed and a light brown crust forms on the bottom of the pot. Stir in ½ cup stock and use it to deglaze (help dissolve) the crust. Stir in the remaining 1 cup stock (take a quick moment to enjoy the wonderful fragrance!) and return the chicken and the accumulated juices to the pot. Bring just to a boil, reduce the heat to low, and simmer for 15 minutes. Add the cheese and the apples. Increase the heat to high and cook, uncovered, stirring every 2 or 3 minutes, for 15 minutes. Stir in the cream, bring just to a boil, then remove from the heat. Serve hot with rice or noodles.

Chicken with Sweet and Sour Cabbage

Photograph No. 8

MAKES 4 SERVINGS

This is a brand-new recipe, but with its colorful combination of apples, red cabbage and caraway seeds, it may remind some of you of dishes popular in Germany and eastern Europe. It's cooked in one large pot, from browning the chicken pieces to the final simmering of all the wonderful ingredients, making it as easy as it is delicious. The sweet-sour liquid is part of the dish, so you don't lose a single nutrient or drop of flavor!

SEASONING MIX

2 teaspoons salt
1 teaspoon caraway seeds
1 teaspoon ground coriander
1 teaspoon dill weed
1 teaspoon ground ginger
1 teaspoon dry mustard
1 teaspoon onion powder

1 teaspoon ground dried Anaheim chile peppers (see pages 1 and 2)
1 teaspoon ground dried pasilla chile peppers (see pages 1 and 2)
½ teaspoon garlic powder
½ teaspoon black pepper
½ teaspoon white pepper
¼ teaspoon ground anise seed

1 (3½- to 4-pound) chicken, cut into 8 pieces
2 tablespoons vegetable oil
2 cups chopped onions, about 1 medium-large (10 ounces)

9 cups red cabbage, cut into ½ inch julienne strips (see page 3), about 1 small head
6 tablespoons sweet rice wine (see page 169)
¼ cup balsamic vinegar

¼ cup cane vinegar (see page 165), or the best, sweetest vinegar you can find

2 large unpeeled tart, crisp apples, such as Granny Smith, cut into large julienne strips (see page 3)

2 cups chicken stock (see pages 5 and 6)

3 tablespoons dark brown sugar

Combine the seasoning mix ingredients in a small bowl and mix well. Sprinkle the chicken pieces evenly with 1 tablespoon plus 1 teaspoon of the seasoning mix and rub it in well.

Heat the oil in a heavy 4-quart pot over high heat just until it begins to smoke, about 3 to 4 minutes. Brown the chicken pieces in batches, large pieces first and skin sides down first, turning several times, about 8 minutes per batch. Remove the chicken—it will not be done at this point, but will finish cooking later—and set it aside. Add the onions, cabbage (the pot will look like it's about to overflow, but the cabbage cooks down quickly), sweet rice wine, balsamic vinegar, cane vinegar (or other variety), apples, the remaining seasoning mix, and the stock. At this point the wonderful fragrance will let everyone know there's something great for dinner! Cook, stirring every 4 or 5 minutes, for 10 minutes, then return the chicken and the accumulated juices to the pot. Bring to a boil, then cover the pot, reduce the heat to medium, and simmer, uncovering to stir every 4 or 5 minutes, for 15 minutes. Uncover and stir in the brown sugar, then cook for 5 minutes longer. Serve piping hot with broad noodles and dark bread for a satisfying and delicious meal.

Holiday Roast Capon

MAKES 4 SERVINGS

Who says you have to wait for a holiday to serve this delicious roast bird? If you feel you must, then make up a special day, like "Yippee! I cleaned out that closet! Day" or "I got my checkbook to balance! Day." As far as I'm concerned, just smelling the aroma of roasting capon or chicken makes it a red-letter day. We've punched up the seasoning with chile peppers, and the combination of mangoes and onions makes the most amazing bird gravy ever! Capon is simply a rooster that has been neutered, allowed to fatten, and marketed while it is still young and tender. Its flavorful meat is especially good for roasting.

2½ teaspoons salt
1½ teaspoons paprika
1 teaspoon ground cumin
1 teaspoon garlic powder
1 teaspoon dry mustard
1 teaspoon onion powder
1 teaspoon ground dried New Mexico
    chile peppers (see pages 1 and 2)

1 teaspoon dried thyme leaves
½ teaspoon cayenne
½ teaspoon black pepper
½ teaspoon white pepper
½ teaspoon ground dried guajillo
    chile peppers (see pages 1 and 2)

1 (4- to 5-pound) capon
2 medium-size chopped ripe mangoes
    (see page 168), about 2 cups

2 cups chopped onions, about 1
    medium-large (10 ounces)

¼ cup cane syrup (see page 165),
    preferred, or pure maple syrup
1 cup heavy cream

Milk or chicken stock (see pages 5
    and 6) if desired to thin gravy

Combine the seasoning mix ingredients in a small bowl and mix well. Rub the outside of the bird with 1 tablespoon plus 1 teaspoon of the seasoning mix, then rub the cavity with 1 tablespoon plus 1 teaspoon of the seasoning mix. Sprinkle *but do not rub in* 1 teaspoon of the seasoning mix evenly over the bird.

Preheat the oven to 225°.

Combine the mangoes, onions and 1 tablespoon of the seasoning mix and stuff the cavity with this mixture. Place the bird on a rack in a roasting pan, breast side up, and place any remaining stuffing on the bottom of the pan, around the edges so as not to interfere with the base of the rack. Roast, uncovered, for 1 hour. Turn the pan 180° (the bird will look barely cooked at this time, but don't worry!), and continue roasting until the bird is done—the internal temperature should be 160°, about 2 to 2½ hours longer.   Insert an oven thermometer into the thickest part of the thigh, along the bone. Reserve the pan drippings for the gravy.

Make the gravy by removing the stuffing from the bird (and the pan if any was placed there) and placing it in a food processor or blender along with the cane syrup (or maple syrup), cream, the pan drippings, and the remaining seasoning mix. Purée until smooth, and if it looks too thick, add a little milk or stock. Serve the gravy as an accompaniment to the roasted bird, and if you have any left over, it's great on sandwiches!

Game Hens Stuffed with Italian Sausage

Photograph No. 9

MAKES 4 SERVINGS

These beautiful stuffed hens make a dramatic presentation for dinner with guests, or to celebrate a special family occasion. If you absolutely can't find kohlrabi, you can substitute turnips, which are almost always available. A special caution: some Italian sausage is very salty, so cook a little of yours and taste it. If it is salty, then reduce the amount of salt in the seasoning mix by 1 teaspoon. I think wild rice or brown rice goes great with these stuffed hens. If your hens have giblets packaged inside, remove them and save for another use.

SEASONING MIX

2 teaspoons paprika
2 teaspoons salt (see above)
1 teaspoon dried basil leaves
1 teaspoon dry mustard
1 teaspoon ground dried Anaheim chile peppers (see pages 1 and 2)
1 teaspoon ground dried New Mexico chile peppers (see pages 1 and 2)

1 teaspoon ground savory
¾ teaspoon cayenne
¾ teaspoon ground cinnamon
¾ teaspoon ground cumin
¾ teaspoon garlic powder
¾ teaspoon onion powder
¼ teaspoon white pepper

4 Cornish game hens, about 5 pounds total
13 ounces fresh Italian sausage (either hot or sweet variety), casings removed
2 cups kohlrabi (see page 168) or turnips, peeled and diced into ½-inch cubes

1½ cups chopped onions, about 1 medium
1 cup chopped yellow bell peppers, about 1 medium
½ cup chopped celery, about 1 stalk
3 tablespoons finely chopped jalapeño chile peppers (see pages 1 and 2)

SAUCE

1 (15-ounce can) tomato sauce
¼ cup minced roasted shallots or small onions (see page 4)

Up to 1 cup chicken stock (see pages 5 and 6)

Combine the seasoning mix ingredients in a small bowl and mix well. Season each bird evenly inside and out with 2 teaspoons of the seasoning mix.

Preheat a heavy 12-inch nonstick skillet over high heat until very hot, about 4 minutes. Add the sausage and cook, stirring and breaking up the sausage as much as possible, until it is nicely browned, about 7 minutes. Drain off and reserve the pan drippings. Add the kohlrabi (or turnips), onions, bell peppers, celery, jalapeño peppers, and the remaining seasoning mix. Cook, stirring every 2 or 3 minutes, until the mixture is browned and begins to stick to the pot, about 12 minutes. Remove from the heat and cool.

Preheat the oven to 250°.

When the stuffing is cool, stuff each bird with about ½ cup of the mixture, reserving 1 cup for the sauce. Close the cavities of the birds with skewers and roast, breast sides up, until done, about 2½ to 3 hours. Keep the hens warm while you make the sauce.

SAUCE In a 10-inch skillet combine the reserved pan drippings with the tomato sauce, reserved stuffing, and the shallots. Bring to a boil, whisking almost constantly, then reduce the heat to low and simmer until slightly thickened, about 15 minutes. (If the sauce thickens too much, whisk in up to 1 cup of stock, return to a boil, and again reduce the heat to low.) Simmer until the sauce reaches the consistency you like, then remove from the heat and serve with the hens.

Duck in a Fresh Fennel Fricassee

MAKES 4 SERVINGS

The dictionary may call fricassee "a dish of poultry or meat cut up, stewed, and served with a rich gravy," but that doesn't begin to do justice to this recipe! No mere "rich gravy" here—we've added a flavorful combination of sweet and white potatoes, fennel bulb, bell peppers and onions, and the seasoning has just the right amount of kick with the chipotle and cayenne peppers. You may have heard the term "cracklings" before and wondered what it meant—now you know. Cracklings are made by frying poultry or pork skin until brown and crisp. Sometimes written as "cracklin's," they're eaten as a snack in the rural South, and by city folks who used to live in the country, like me.

SEASONING MIX

1¾ teaspoons salt
1½ teaspoons paprika
1 teaspoon dried chervil leaves
1 teaspoon ground cinnamon
1 teaspoon ground cumin
1 teaspoon garlic powder
1 teaspoon ground ginger
1 teaspoon dry mustard

1 teaspoon onion powder
1 teaspoon ground dried chipotle
   chile peppers (see pages 1 and 2)
½ teaspoon cayenne
½ teaspoon black pepper
¼ teaspoon ground mace
¼ teaspoon white pepper

1 (4- to 5-pound) duck, cut into 8
  pieces
1 cup chopped onions, about 1
  small (5 ounces)
1½ cups fennel bulb, trimmed and
  diced into ½-inch cubes, in all
2 cups sweet potatoes, peeled and
  diced into ½-inch cubes, about 1

medium-small (10 or 11 ounces),
  in all
½ cup chopped green bell peppers,
  about ½ medium
4 cups duck stock or chicken stock
  (see pages 5 and 6), in all
2 cups white potatoes, peeled and
  diced into ½-inch cubes, about 1
  medium-large (12 or 13 ounces)

Combine the seasoning mix ingredients in a small bowl and mix well.

Remove the skin and all visible fat from the duck pieces, finely dice the skin and fat and place it in a heavy 6-inch skillet, preferably nonstick, over low heat. If you cook the skin too fast, you might run the risk of burning it without rendering the fat. Cook until the skin and fat pieces are nicely browned and have rendered their fat, about 20 minutes. If there is a lot of fat, you may want to drain it off midway through this process, so that all the skin can brown. Pour the skin and fat through a strainer into a small bowl. Reserve 2 tablespoons of the duck fat (save the rest for another use—add to cooking oil for a great flavor, and it will keep for up to a month), and set aside the browned and drained skin (cracklings).

Sprinkle the duck pieces with 1 tablespoon of the seasoning mix and rub it in well.

In a heavy 4-quart pot over high heat, heat the reserved fat until it is very hot, about 4 minutes. Cook the seasoned duck pieces in batches, large pieces first, turning several times, until they are a rich golden brown but not cooked through. Remove the duck from the pot and set it aside. To the pot add the onions, 1 cup of the fennel, 1 cup of the sweet potatoes, and the bell peppers. Scrape the pot well, allowing the liquid from the vegetables to help deglaze (dissolve the browned bits) the pot bottom. If the brown pieces stick so hard that you can hardly scrape them up, add a little stock and scrape well. Cook, stirring once or twice, for 5 minutes, then add 1 tablespoon of the seasoning mix. Cook, stirring and scraping the pot bottom 2 or 3 times, for 8 minutes. Add ½ cup stock and scrape the pot bottom well, then add the remaining seasoning mix and the white potatoes. Cover and cook, stirring and scraping every 2 minutes, for 8 minutes. Stir in 2½ cups stock and cook for 3 minutes longer.

With a potato masher or a heavy slotted spoon, smash the mixture against the sides and bottom of the pot, mashing the potatoes until the liquid becomes thick and the bubbles resemble little volcanoes, about 4 minutes. Whisk in the remaining stock, then return the duck and the accumulated juices to the pot. Cover, bring just to a boil, then reduce the heat to low and simmer for 20 minutes. Add the remaining sweet potatoes and the remaining fennel and simmer, covered, for 30 minutes. Add the cracklings, remove from the heat, and serve.

SWIMMING STUFF

STUFF

FROM THE SEVEN SEAS

Bronzed Trout with a Mango-Spinach Purée

Photograph No. 10

MAKES 4 SERVINGS

Bronzed fish is a treat all alone, but here we've added a wonderful purée of spinach and mango, with cream and good seasonings—the dill weed, for instance, really enhances the other herbs. Serve this with the freshest spring asparagus in the market or French-cut green beans and perhaps a bit of Honey Mustard Corn Chow-Chow (page 45) for a very impressive dinner that's easy to prepare. You can use this recipe with any firm-fleshed white fish, such as orange roughy or tilapia. See page 47 for a complete description of bronzing.

SEASONING MIX

1 teaspoon paprika	½ teaspoon onion powder
1 teaspoon salt	½ teaspoon ground dried ancho chile
¾ teaspoon dill weed	peppers (see pages 1 and 2)
¾ teaspoon ground ginger	¼ teaspoon cayenne
½ teaspoon ground cumin	¼ teaspoon black pepper
½ teaspoon garlic powder	

4 trout fillets, about 8 ounces each	1 very ripe medium-size mango,
4 teaspoons unsalted butter, in all	about 12 ounces (see page 168),
½ cup chopped onions, about ½	chopped, about 1 to 1½ cups of
small (2½ ounces)	pulp
5 ounces spinach leaves, washed	1½ cups fish stock (see page 6), in
and drained, stems removed,	all
and torn into pieces	½ cup sour cream (see page 3)

Combine the seasoning mix ingredients in a small bowl and mix well.

In an 8-inch nonstick skillet over medium-high heat, melt 2 tablespoons of the butter, about 3 minutes, then add the onions. Cook until the onions are just beginning to turn brown, about 6 minutes, and add the spinach. Cook, stirring almost constantly, until the spinach wilts, about 3 minutes. Add the mango pulp and 2 teaspoons of the seasoning mix. Cook until the mango just begins to brown and stick to the skillet, about 4 minutes. Stir in 1 cup of stock, then stir and scrape the mixture thoroughly, loosening all the brown bits from the bottom of the skillet.

Remove from the heat and transfer the mixture to a food processor or blender and purée, then return it to the skillet over medium-high heat.

Whisk in the remaining ½ cup stock and the sour cream. Bring the mixture to a boil, stirring constantly, and when it begins to sputter like little volcanoes, remove from the heat and set aside.

Preheat a 12-inch nonstick skillet over high heat until very hot, about 5 minutes.

Melt the remaining butter. Place 2 of the fillets on a plate and brush one side of each with the melted butter. Sprinkle each buttered side with ½ teaspoon of the seasoning mix and place both fillets, buttered and seasoned sides down, in the hot skillet. Brush the top sides with melted butter and season each with ½ teaspoon of the seasoning mix. Cook, turning twice, until both sides are a rich golden brown and just cooked through, about 3 to 4 minutes in all. Remove from the skillet and keep warm in a 200° oven while you cook the remaining fillets. To serve, spread ½ cup of the purée on each plate and carefully place a fillet on top of the purée.

Fresh Tuna and Lima Bean Salad

MAKES 4 SERVINGS

Oyster mushrooms, which are an important ingredient in this recipe, are often sold in large clumps. If yours come this way, pull the individual mushrooms off by hand, then dice the remaining clump. If you absolutely cannot find oyster mushrooms, you can still make the salad by substituting any fresh white mushrooms. Fresh lima beans also may be hard to find; their taste and texture are definitely worth the search, but if they're not available, use a good brand of frozen limas. This recipe makes generous servings—I like it for lunch with toasted thin slices of bagels. It's a versatile recipe, too, because you can use any fresh vegetables you like in the cooked vegetable mixture—just be sure to dice them into ¼-inch cubes—and your favorite fresh greens to form the bed of leaves.

SEASONING MIX

1½ teaspoons paprika	¾ teaspoon ground cumin
1½ teaspoons salt	¾ teaspoon garlic powder
1¼ teaspoons ground ginger	¾ teaspoon dry mustard
1¼ teaspoons onion powder	½ teaspoon cayenne
1 teaspoon ground dried Anaheim	½ teaspoon black pepper
chile peppers (see pages 1 and 2)	¼ teaspoon white pepper

4 (6-inch diameter) corn tortillas
Vegetable oil for frying
3 cups seafood stock (see page 6)
2 tablespoons lightly packed dark
  brown sugar
1 pound fresh lima beans, about 3
  cups
1 cup carrots, diced into ¼-inch
  cubes
1 cup onions, diced into ¼-inch
  cubes, about 1 small (5 ounces)
1 small (6 ounces) turnip, diced
  into ¼-inch cubes, about 1 scant
  cup

2 medium fresh tomatoes, peeled
  (see page 7) and chopped, about
  1½ cups
¼ cup fresh poblano chile peppers
  (see pages 1 and 2), diced into
  ¼-inch cubes
1 teaspoon minced fresh garlic,
  about 1 clove
3 fresh tuna steaks, about 6 to 8
  ounces each
Radicchio or lettuce leaves for
  serving
¼ cup thinly sliced green onions,
  about 3 stalks

Combine the seasoning mix ingredients in a small bowl and mix well.

Pour enough vegetable oil into a 10-inch skillet to measure 1 inch deep and place over high heat until the oil begins to smoke, about 6 to 7 minutes. Fry the tortillas, turning once or twice, until they are brown and crispy. When the oil stops bubbling, the moisture has evaporated from the tortillas—a sure sign they are done. Drain the tortillas on paper towels, and when they are cool enough to handle, break them into pieces and pulverize them in a food processor. Or you can pulverize the tortillas by placing them in a strong unsealed plastic bag and crushing them with a rolling pin. Set aside.

Place the stock in a 3-quart pot over high heat, cover, and bring to a boil. Uncover and stir in 2 tablespoons of the seasoning mix and the brown sugar. Re-cover and cook for 4 minutes, then uncover and add the lima beans. Re-cover and cook until the beans are tender, about 9 or 10 minutes. Uncover and add the carrots, onions, turnip, poblanos, and garlic, and cook, covered, for 4 minutes. Uncover and stir in the tomatoes. Cover, bring just to a boil, then remove from the heat. Strain off the vegetables, reserving both the vegetables and the liquid. Transfer the vegetables to a platter and set aside to cool.

Return the liquid to the pot, place over high heat, and bring to a boil. Cook until the liquid is reduced to ½ cup, about 6 to 8 minutes, and set aside for use in the mayonnaise.

Prepare the Oyster Mushroom Mayonnaise (recipe follows).

Sprinkle each side of each tuna steak evenly with ½ teaspoon of the seasoning mix and gently pat it in.

Heat a 10- or 12-inch cast iron skillet over high heat until it is extremely hot, about 10 minutes. Place the tuna steaks in the dry skillet and cook, turning once, until the seasoning mix is very dark brown and the tuna steaks are browned and opaque on the outside but still red and rare inside, about 1½ minutes per side. If you cook the tuna until it's "done" all the way through, or white, it will be very dry. Remove the tuna steaks from the skillet, and when they are cool enough to handle, break them apart with a fork into ½-inch pieces.

Arrange a bed of radicchio or lettuce—three to six leaves, depending on their size—on each serving plate and spread ¼ of the bean mixture, about 1½ cups, evenly on the lettuce. Add ¼ of the crumbled tuna, about 6 ounces, and, without covering the tuna, drizzle about ½ cup of the Oyster Mushroom Mayonnaise over the salad. Top each serving with 1 tablespoon green onions and a sprinkling of the tortilla crumbs. Serve at once.

Oyster Mushroom Mayonnaise

1 large egg
2 tablespoons apple cider vinegar
½ cup vegetable oil (see note below)
½ cup extra-virgin olive oil

½ cup reserved, reduced cooking liquid
2 cups oyster mushrooms, trimmed, washed, separated, and diced into ¼-inch pieces

Place the vegetable oil and the olive oil in a measuring cup and stir until thoroughly combined.

Process the egg and vinegar in a blender just until it is light and frothy, about 30 seconds. With the blender on, slowly add the oils in a thin stream until the oil is absorbed and a thick mayonnaise consistency is reached, about 30 seconds longer. Add the reduced cooking liquid, the mushrooms, and 1 teaspoon of the seasoning mix, and stir gently with a rubber spatula until thoroughly blended. Refrigerate leftover mayonnaise.

NOTE: Because the size of eggs varies, you may need to use a little more or a little less oil to achieve the proper mayonnaise consistency.

Salmon Pudding with a Portobello Glaze

Photograph No. 11

MAKES 4 SERVINGS

In this recipe we introduce you to a different way of cooking fish steaks—on one side only. Let me tell you why: as the fish cooks in the pan without turning, the heat forces the liquid to the top, where it's about 170°. At that temperature the fish retains most of its liquid, so when it's done it's still very moist and flavorful, almost like a pudding.

If you cannot find boneless salmon steaks, or your butcher will not trim them for you, here is how to trim them yourself—looking at the center of the salmon steak, find the backbone and cut around it with a small knife, following close to the bone and being careful not to cut through the skin. Remove the backbone and press gently with your fingers on both sides of the steak, feeling for any remaining bones. Pull the remaining bones out with your fingers or a small pair of pliers. If there is any white membrane remaining on the inside edges of the salmon, trim it off as well. Also, salmon is one of the very few fish varieties that besides oil has fat between the flesh and skin. If this fat gets above 50° it starts to smell "fishy" after a couple of days, so unless your salmon is fresh out of the water, it's best to cut all the fat away. If you don't remove the fat, the fish would still taste OK when you cook it, but it would smell bad.

SEASONING MIX

1¼ teaspoons salt
¾ teaspoon dried basil leaves
¾ teaspoon garlic powder
¾ teaspoon onion powder
½ teaspoon cayenne
½ teaspoon paprika
½ teaspoon black pepper

½ teaspoon ground dried Anaheim chile peppers (see pages 1 and 2)
½ teaspoon ground turmeric
¼ teaspoon white pepper
¼ teaspoon ground dried chipotle chile peppers (see pages 1 and 2)

4 boneless salmon steaks, skin on, each about 10 ounces and 1 inch thick
4 tablespoons unsalted butter, in all
1½ cups chopped onions, about 1 medium-small

2 cups portobello mushroom (see page 169), diced into 1-inch cubes, about 1 mushroom with a 5-inch diameter
½ cup mashed baked sweet potato, about 1 (4-ounce) potato
1½ cups fish stock or seafood stock (see page 6), in all

Combine the seasoning mix ingredients in a small bowl and mix well.

Sprinkle only one side of each salmon steak with 1 teaspoon of the seasoning mix and gently pat it in.

Cut off 4 teaspoons (1 tablespoon plus 1 teaspoon) of the butter, and divide each teaspoon into 5 pieces.

Place the butter pieces on the bottom of a cold 12-inch skillet, then place the salmon steaks, seasoned sides down, in the skillet on top of the butter. Place the skillet on the stove and turn on the heat to very low. Cook, without covering or turning, until the tops of the steaks are just beginning to become warm and darken slightly, and the inside edges of the steaks are soft and white almost to the top, about 30 minutes.

While the salmon is cooking, make the glaze (recipe follows).

Portobello Glaze

In a 4-quart pot over high heat, melt 1 tablespoon plus 2 teaspoons of butter. As soon as it sizzles add the onions and cook, stirring constantly, until the onions are browning at the edges, about 10 minutes. Add the mushrooms and the remaining 1 tablespoon butter and cook, stirring constantly, for 3 minutes. Stir in 2 teaspoons seasoning mix and continue to cook until the mushrooms are dark and the onions are turning dark brown at the edges, about 2 minutes. Add ½ cup stock and scrape the bottom of the pot to loosen any brown bits. Add the sweet potato and ½ cup stock. Remove from the heat and purée in a food processor or blender. Return the puréed mixture to the pot over high heat. Whisk in the remaining ½ cup stock and ½ teaspoon seasoning mix and bring the mixture to a boil. When the boiling is brisk and the bubbles are shooting up in small streams, remove from the heat.

For each serving, spoon ½ cup of the glaze on a plate and top with a salmon steak.

Red Snapper with Crawfish Dressing

MAKES 4 SERVINGS

Here's a dish that's popular in homes and restaurants all over south Louisiana. It looks very impressive, but read the recipe over and you'll see that the preparation is not difficult at all. As with all fish and seafood, you want to buy the freshest products possible and cook them the same day. I think it's a good idea to shop where the fish are displayed whole, so you can check to be sure the eyes are bright and clear (a reliable sign of freshness), and have them filleted, rather than buying fish that have already been filleted. You can substitute 1 pound small peeled shrimp (40 to 50 count, see page 4) for the crawfish if you prefer.

SEASONING MIX

2¼ teaspoons salt
1¾ teaspoons dill weed
1¾ teaspoons onion powder
1¼ teaspoons ground fenugreek (see page 167)
1¼ teaspoons garlic powder
1¼ teaspoons ground ginger
1 teaspoon dry mustard

1 teaspoon ground dried Anaheim chile peppers (see pages 1 and 2)
1 teaspoon ground dried pasilla chile peppers (see pages 1 and 2)
¾ teaspoon cayenne
¾ teaspoon ground cumin
½ teaspoon black pepper
½ teaspoon ground savory
¼ teaspoon white pepper

2 red snapper fillets, about 1 pound each
5 tablespoons olive oil, in all
1 pound crawfish tails with fat, or small shrimp
1½ cups chopped onions, about 1 medium (6 to 7 ounces)
10 medium-sized peeled whole garlic cloves
1½ cups chopped red bell peppers, about 1½ medium
¾ cup chopped fresh poblano chile peppers (see pages 1 and 2)

1½ tablespoons finely chopped fresh fennel leaves (see page 167)
1½ cups fish stock (see page 6), in all
2 cups white potatoes, peeled and diced into ½-inch cubes, about 1 medium-large (12 to 13 ounces)
1½ cups mirliton (see page 169), peeled and diced into ½-inch cubes, about 1 medium (10 ounces)
6 tablespoons unsalted butter, in all
1 tablespoon light brown sugar

Combine the seasoning mix ingredients in a small bowl and mix well.

Sprinkle each side of each snapper fillet with ¾ teaspoon of the seasoning mix and gently pat it in.

Reserve 20 of the best-looking crawfish (or shrimp) for decoration and finely chop the remainder.

In a 4-quart pot over high heat, heat 2 tablespoons of the olive oil just until it begins to smoke, about 3 to 4 minutes. Add the onions and garlic cloves and cook, stirring at 2 minute intervals, until the onions are wilted and beginning to brown, about 4 minutes. Add the bell peppers and the poblano chilies and cook, stirring every 2 minutes, until the mixture begins to stick slightly, about 10 minutes. Stir in 1 tablespoon plus 2 teaspoons of the seasoning mix and the fennel, then stir in 1 cup of the stock, the potatoes, and mirlitons. Cover and cook, uncovering every 2 minutes to stir the pot and check to be sure the mixture is not sticking. When the mixture is thickened and begins to stick again, about 15 minutes, add the remaining ½ cup stock and scrape the bottom well. Cover and cook, uncovering to stir every 2 minutes, for an additional 8 minutes. Remove from the heat and stir in 3 tablespoons of the butter, the brown sugar, the remaining olive oil, and 1 tablespoon plus 1½ teaspoons of the seasoning mix. Stir until the mixture is well blended and the butter melts completely.

Purée the mixture in a food processor or blender until very smooth, then spread the mixture on a sheet pan and refrigerate until cold. Combine the mixture with the chopped crawfish (or shrimp) and stir until evenly mixed.

Preheat the oven to 350°.

Cut the remaining 3 tablespoons of butter into very thin slices. Place the fillets on a baking sheet with ½ of the thinly sliced butter under each fillet. Using a pastry bag fitted with a large star point, pipe ½ of the mixture onto each fillet, covering the fillet evenly. Or, if you prefer, simply spread the mixture evenly on the fish. Place 10 of the reserved crawfish (or shrimp) in a line down the center of each fillet. Bake until the fish is cooked through but still moist and tender, about 12 to 15 minutes, and serve immediately.

Charlotte's Crawfish Wraps

MAKES 24 ROLLS, ENOUGH FOR 6 TO 8 APPETIZER SERVINGS

An Oriental idea—using Greek pastry, all-American mashed potatoes, and Louisiana crawfish—produces not a collection, but an international delight! In the unlikely event you have some of these delicious rolls left over, they reheat easily in a hot oven for a few minutes. You also can make them ahead, cover them with plastic wrap then a damp cloth, and cook just as you're ready to serve.

If you've never used phyllo sheets before, be sure to read the package directions for proper handling before you begin—they're easy to work with, but they do require care. Handle them gently to avoid tearing, and keep them from drying out. The brand we use comes in one-pound packages that contain "about" 20 sheets of dough, each 14 inches by 18 inches, which would give you 120 rectangles the size we call for. Even allowing for tearing some, you're still going to have some left over, which is great, because you can experiment with pastries and other fillings. You can substitute small boiled shrimp for the crawfish tails if you prefer.

Charlotte Livingston is the vivacious daughter of Patricia Livingston, our editor who also tests all the recipes in her home kitchen. Charlotte told us her two favorite foods in the whole world are crawfish and egg rolls, so when we combined the two, she was in heaven! I'm surprised Patricia didn't accidentally-on-purpose mess up the recipe, so she'd have to do it again and again.

SEASONING MIX

1½ teaspoons salt
1 teaspoon paprika
1 teaspoon onion powder
¾ teaspoon dried basil leaves
¾ teaspoon garlic powder
¾ teaspoon ground ginger
½ teaspoon cayenne

½ teaspoon ground coriander
½ teaspoon ground dried árbol chile
   peppers (see pages 1 and 2)
¼ teaspoon ground allspice
¼ teaspoon black pepper
¼ teaspoon white pepper

3 cups white potatoes, peeled, cooked and diced into 1-inch cubes, about 2 medium (10 ounces each)
6 tablespoons heavy cream
3 tablespoons chicken stock (see pages 5 and 6)
1 tablespoon unsalted butter
8 cloves roasted garlic (see page 4), peeled and minced
½ pound peeled crawfish tails or small peeled shrimp (40-50 count, see page 4)

½ teaspoon minced fresh serrano chile peppers (see pages 1 and 2)
1 tablespoon minced fresh poblano chile peppers (see pages 1 and 2)
2 cups vegetable oil
72 rectangles phyllo dough (see page 170), each about 6 inches by 7 inches
2 large eggs, lightly beaten with 2 tablespoons water

Combine the seasoning mix ingredients in a small bowl and mix well.

In a large bowl, combine the cooked potatoes, cream, stock, butter, roasted garlic, and the seasoning mix, and mash thoroughly with a potato masher. Combine the potato mixture with the crawfish, serrano chilies and poblano chilies. Stir gently until evenly mixed.

Heat the oil to 350° in a large skillet. Use a cooking thermometer and adjust the heat so the temperature of the oil remains as steady as possible. An electric skillet, if you have one, works great.

Lightly brush 3 phyllo squares with the egg wash and stack them.

Place ¼ cup of the stuffing diagonally across the stack, fold one corner of the squares over the stuffing and press gently to firm the stuffing, turn in the corners, and roll up like an egg roll. Continue with the remaining squares and stuffing to form all the rolls. Cook in the hot oil, as many rolls at a time as your skillet will hold without crowding, turning as necessary, until golden-brown on all sides, about 4 to 8 minutes. Remove each roll from the oil as it's done, and drain on paper towels.

Serve with a sweet and sour dipping sauce, tamari, or hot mustard sauce.

Soft Shell Crabs with Adobo Sauce

MAKES 4 APPETIZER SERVINGS OR 2 MAIN-COURSE SERVINGS

Soft shell crabs are delicate creatures, and they should always be handled gently to avoid breaking or tearing them. To clean a soft shell crab place it in front of you, legs down. Cut off the eyes and the tip of the mouth. Gently lift up one side of the shell, exposing the gills, which are a row of feather-like objects. Some people in Louisiana call them "dead men" or "dead men's fingers." Remove the gills and close the shell. Repeat this process on the other side. Turn the crab over and locate the "apron," which is a piece shaped like a handle on male crabs and like a bell on females. Pull off the apron and the membranes attaching it to the crab.

SEASONING MIX

2 teaspoons salt
1½ teaspoons garlic powder
1½ teaspoons paprika
1 teaspoon ground cumin
1 teaspoon ground dried Anaheim
  chile peppers (see pages 1 and 2)
1 teaspoon ground dried ancho chile
  peppers (see pages 1 and 2)

1 teaspoon ground dried New Mexico
  chile peppers (see pages 1 and 2)
¾ teaspoon onion powder
½ teaspoon cayenne
½ teaspoon black pepper
¼ teaspoon white pepper

4 soft shell crabs, about 5 ounces
  each, cleaned (see above)

1½ cups all purpose-flour
1½ cups vegetable oil

Combine the seasoning mix ingredients in a small bowl and mix well.

Season each side of each crab with ¾ teaspoon of the seasoning mix.

Combine the flour with 1 tablespoon of the seasoning mix in a cake pan or casserole dish with 1-inch sides.

In a 12-inch nonstick skillet over high heat, heat the oil to 325°, about 15 minutes.

Dredge 1 crab in the seasoned flour, coating it completely, then gently shake off the excess. *Immediately* transfer the crab to the hot oil and cook, turning once, until golden brown and crisp on both sides, about 4 to 5 minutes per side. Place it on a warm ceramic platter large enough to hold all four crabs, and repeat until all the crabs are cooked.

Pour off and discard the oil from the skillet, leaving as much of the browned flour as possible, and keep the crabs warm in a 200° oven while you make the sauce.

Adobo Sauce

2 tablespoons unsalted butter, in all
½ cup crab stock or seafood stock (see page 6)
¼ cup fresh lime juice
3 tablespoons canned chipotle chilies in adobo, finely chopped, plus 2 tablespoons of the adobo liquid
1 (4.25-ounce) can chopped mild green chilies
1 tablespoon minced fresh garlic, about 3 cloves
2 teaspoons light brown sugar

Return the skillet to high heat and add the stock, lime juice, chipotle chilies and adobo liquid, green chilies, garlic, and the remaining seasoning mix. Whisk well to combine, then bring to a boil. Add the brown sugar and continue simmering, whisking constantly, for 2 minutes, then remove from the heat. Add the butter and whisk gently until the butter melts and is absorbed. Transfer to a blender or food processor, and purée for 30 seconds.

Divide the Adobo Sauce among the crabs and serve immediately.

French Quarter Eggplant

Photograph No. 12

MAKES 4 SERVINGS

Variations of this dish are found in many New Orleans restaurants, where it's popular with locals as well as visitors. And no wonder—the combination of fresh shrimp, well-seasoned vegetables, and a great sauce is irresistible! The sauce, made from three varieties of squash, forms the base for the "rafts," eggplant slices coated with flour and bread crumbs, then quickly fried to golden-brown perfection. Next up is the stuffing, similar to the sauce, but with its flavors enhanced by onions, bell peppers and celery, then the whole is topped with perfectly fried butterfly shrimp. I know it sounds a little complicated, but it really isn't, so just follow the step-by-step directions, and you'll produce a wonderful and dramatic-looking lunch or light supper.

SEASONING MIX

1 tablespoon plus ¾ teaspoon salt
2½ teaspoons dried oregano leaves
2 teaspoons onion powder
2 teaspoons dried thyme leaves
1¾ teaspoons dried basil leaves
1¼ teaspoons garlic powder
1¼ teaspoons paprika

1¼ teaspoons dried tarragon leaves
1 teaspoon cayenne
1 teaspoon ground cumin
¾ teaspoon dry mustard
¾ teaspoon white pepper
¾ teaspoon black pepper

1 large eggplant, preferably round
   rather than long

STUFFING MIXTURE

2 cups butternut squash, peeled
   and diced into ¼-inch cubes,
   about 1 small squash
1¼ cups zucchini, peeled and diced
   into ¼- inch cubes, about 1
   medium-size squash
1¼ cups yellow squash, scrubbed
   and diced into ¼-inch cubes,
   about 2 small squash
2 cups chopped onions, about 1
   medium-large (10 ounces)

2 cups chopped green bell peppers,
   about 2 medium
1 cup chopped celery, about 2
   stalks
1 teaspoon minced fresh garlic,
   about 1 clove
4 teaspoons unsalted butter
¾ cup vegetable stock or seafood
   stock (see pages 5 and 6)

SAUCE

2 tablespoons unsalted butter
2 cups heavy cream

½ cup milk, if needed

RAFTS AND SHRIMP

6 cups vegetable oil
2 cups all-purpose flour
2 large eggs
1 cup milk

1 cup unseasoned bread crumbs
32 peeled shrimp, 21 to 25 count
   (see page 4), deveined

Combine the seasoning mix ingredients in a small bowl and mix well.

Peel the eggplant, then cut a piece about ½ inch thick off one side and
set the piece aside.

Starting from the flat side, cut four ½-inch slices and set them aside.
Dice the remaining trimmings (including the first small piece you cut)
into ¼-inch pieces and reserve.

Season each side of each eggplant slice with ½ teaspoon of the seasoning mix and set them aside.

STUFFING MIXTURE Combine the butternut squash, zucchini, and yellow squash and reserve a cup of this mixture for the sauce.

Preheat a heavy 5-quart pot over high heat until very hot, 4 to 5 minutes. To the pot add the diced eggplant, remaining mixed squash, all the onions, bell peppers, celery, and garlic. Place the butter on top of the vegetables and stir, allowing the butter to melt slowly. When the butter melts, add 2 tablespoons plus 2 teaspoons of the seasoning mix. Stir well, cover and cook, stirring and scraping the bottom of the pot every 4 to 5 minutes, for 20 minutes. Add the stock and scrape the pot bottom completely. Cook, stirring every 3 minutes, for 9 minutes, and remove from the heat.

SAUCE Combine the set-aside cup of mixed squash, the butter, and the cream in a blender and process until smooth, about 1 minute. Transfer to an 8-inch skillet, add 1 tablespoon plus 1 teaspoon of the seasoning mix, and bring to a boil over high heat . If the mixture makes bubbles like little volcanoes that splatter, it is too thick. If that occurs add the milk in ¼-cup increments until the sauce reaches the right consistency. Reduce the heat to low and simmer, stirring almost constantly, until the mixture is thick, about 15 minutes. Be careful not to let the mixture stick to the skillet bottom, as it will burn very easily.

RAFTS In a 5-quart pot heat the oil to 350°.

Place the flour in a shallow pan. In a similar pan, whisk the eggs and milk together until thoroughly combined. Place the bread crumbs in a third pan. Dredge the eggplant slices in the flour, press the flour onto the surfaces, put the eggplant into the egg wash, making sure that the flour is completely moistened. Next, place the eggplant slices in the bread crumbs, scoop up some of the bread crumbs and gently press them into the eggplant so they will stick, and transfer *immediately* to the hot oil and fry, turning frequently, until golden brown, about 5 minutes. Drain on paper towels.

SHRIMP Butterfly the front halves (cut down the middles and press open with your fingers) of the shrimp, leaving the tail halves uncut. Season all the shrimp with the remaining seasoning mix, working the seasonings in evenly with your hands. Dredge the shrimp in the flour, press the flour onto the surfaces of the shrimp, then put them into the egg wash, making sure that the flour is completely moistened. Next, place them into the flour again and gently press with more flour, making sure that the shrimp are coated with flour. Transfer *immediately* to the hot oil and fry until they are golden brown and look crisp, which takes less than 1 minute. Drain on paper towels.

ASSEMBLY Divide the sauce among 4 serving plates. Place an eggplant slice on the sauce in each of the plates, divide the stuffing among the portions, and top each with 6 to 8 shrimp. Serve at once and enjoy!

SIDE BY SIDE.

TRAVELIN' TOGETHER

Mandeville Street Rice

MAKES 11 CUPS

A special rice like this one adds immeasurably to your dinner, either as a side dish or, since it contains meat, as a main course. Fair warning, though—it's a little peppery, so reduce the amount of cayenne and chipotle if you're serving someone who can't handle the heat. Parsnips, which look a lot like white carrots, are under-utilized in this country, even though they've been here as long as the Pilgrims!

SEASONING MIX

1 tablespoon salt
2 teaspoons ground cumin
2 teaspoons garlic powder
2 teaspoons paprika
1½ teaspoons cayenne
1½ teaspoons dry mustard

1½ teaspoons black pepper
1½ teaspoons dried thyme leaves
1 teaspoon onion powder
1 teaspoon ground dried chipotle
    chile peppers (see pages 1 and 2)

2 tablespoons olive oil
2 cups chopped onions, about 2
    small (5 ounces each)
2 cups chopped green bell peppers,
    about 2 medium
3 bay leaves
1 pound ground beef

4 cups parsnips (see page 170),
    peeled and diced into ½-inch
    pieces
2 cups chopped red bell peppers,
    about 2 medium
6 cups beef stock (see page 6)
3 cups uncooked Converted® rice
    (see page 170)

Combine the seasoning mix ingredients in a small bowl and mix well.

In a 5-quart pot over high heat, heat the oil just until it begins to smoke, about 3 to 4 minutes. Add the onions, green bell peppers, bay leaves and 2 tablespoons of the seasoning mix. Cook, stirring every 2 minutes, for 8 minutes. Push the vegetables to one side of the pot, then add the ground meat and the remaining seasoning mix. Cook, stirring and breaking up the clumps of meat, until the meat is browned, about 10 minutes, then add the parsnips. Cover and cook, uncovering every 2 minutes to stir and scrape the bottom of the pot, for 10 minutes. Add the red bell peppers and stock. Cover, bring to a boil, then uncover and add the rice. Reduce the heat to very low and simmer gently, tightly covered, until the rice absorbs most of the liquid, about 20 minutes. Remove from the heat and let sit for 10 minutes before serving. This rice dish is intended to be slightly moist.

Kohlrabi Rice Extraordinaire

MAKES 10 SIDE-DISH SERVINGS

We listed this tasty recipe as a side dish because it's so great with ham steaks or roast pork. On the other hand it's almost a meal-in-one-dish because it has meat, vegetable, and starch. However you serve it, it's sure to be a favorite with your family and friends. Some of the spices we've used, like cinnamon and nutmeg, are more usually found in desserts, but I think they really enhance the kohlrabi or turnips. It's really important that the ham, onions, and kohlrabi all be diced the same size, about ¼ inch.

SEASONING MIX

1¼ teaspoons salt
¾ teaspoon garlic powder
¾ teaspoon dry mustard
¾ teaspoon onion powder
¾ teaspoon paprika
½ teaspoon cayenne
½ teaspoon ground coriander

½ teaspoon ground dried árbol chile peppers (see pages 1 and 2)
¼ teaspoon ground cinnamon
¼ teaspoon ground ginger
¼ teaspoon ground nutmeg
¼ teaspoon black pepper
¼ teaspoon white pepper

2 tablespoons vegetable oil
½ pound top-quality pre-cooked lean ham, diced into ¼-inch cubes
2 cups onions, diced into ¼-inch cubes, about 2 medium (5 ounces each)

2 cups kohlrabi (see page 168) or turnips, peeled and diced into ¼-inch cubes (about 12 ounces)
1 teaspoon minced fresh garlic, about 1 clove
4 cups chicken stock (see pages 5 and 6)
2 cups Converted® rice

Combine the seasoning mix ingredients in a small bowl and mix well.

In a heavy 4-quart pot over high heat, heat the oil just until it begins to smoke, about 3 to 4 minutes. Add the ham, onions, kohlrabi (or turnips), garlic, and seasoning mix. Cook, stirring and scraping the pot every 4 to 5 minutes, until the mixture begins to stick hard to the bottom and sides of the pot, about 12 minutes—watch carefully and be sure not to let the mixture burn. If your pot is not very thick, or if your stove puts out an unusual amount of heat, lower the heat a little bit if necessary. At the end of the 12 minutes, stir in the stock and rice, cover the pot and bring the mixture just to a boil—you'll know when it begins to boil when little puffs of steam escape from under the lid. Reduce the heat to low and simmer (without peeking!) until all the liquid is absorbed, about 20 minutes. Remove from the heat and let sit, covered, for 10 minutes before serving.

Tasso-Stuffed White Squash

Photograph No. 9

MAKES 4 SERVINGS

Mrs. Podunk says she just loves this dish because although the seasoning is complex and distinctive, it's not too hot! It's an easy recipe to double, so you can serve twice as many people with no extra effort, and you can make it vegetarian by omitting the tasso (add a little diced carrot instead and change the name of the recipe) and using only vegetable stock. The ladies tell me it looks nice served on a clean squash leaf or two with a squash blossom, if available, on the side. By the way, white squash is also called summer squash or patty pan squash.

SEASONING MIX

2 teaspoons salt
1 teaspoon ground coriander
1 teaspoon garlic powder
1 teaspoon dry mustard
¾ teaspoon ground cumin
¾ teaspoon ground nutmeg

¾ teaspoon black pepper
¾ teaspoon ground dried pasilla
　chile peppers (see pages 1 and 2)
½ teaspoon ground ginger
½ teaspoon white pepper

5 large white squashes
2 tablespoons olive oil
4 ounces tasso (see page 172) or
　smoked ham, diced into ¼-inch
　cubes
1 cup chopped onions, about 1
　small (5 ounces)
½ cup chopped red bell peppers,
　about ½ medium
½ cup chopped yellow bell
　peppers, about ½ medium

2 cups white potatoes, peeled and
　diced into ½-inch cubes, about 1
　large (13 ounces)
3¾ cups vegetable stock or
　chicken stock (see pages 5 and
　6), in all
2 cups sweet potatoes, peeled and
　diced into ½-inch cubes, about 1
　medium-small (11 ounces), in all
½ cup heavy cream

Combine the seasoning mix ingredients in a small bowl and mix well.

Peel and finely dice 1 squash, and set it aside.

Carefully remove a circular section from the stem end of each of the remaining 4 squashes, angling the cuts inward as when cutting the top of a pumpkin. Scoop out the soft centers and seeds and set aside. With a spoon or a melon baller, scrape out as much of the white flesh as possible without breaking through the skins. Combine the squash flesh with the soft pulp, then chop and combine with the diced squash and set aside. Parboil the shells in rapidly boiling water for 5 minutes, drain, and set them aside.

In a heavy 12-inch nonstick skillet over high heat, heat the oil just until it begins to smoke, about 3 to 4 minutes. Add all the diced squash and pulp, the tasso, onions, bell peppers, white potatoes, 1 cup of the sweet potatoes, and 2 tablespoons of the seasoning mix. Stir well, then cover and cook until the vegetables are browned on the bottom, about 6 to 8 minutes. Uncover and stir, then re-cover and cook until the vegetables brown again and are soft and the potatoes are cooked through, about 16 to 20 minutes. Uncover and stir in ¾ cup stock and cook, stirring and scraping almost constantly, until the mixture absorbs the stock and becomes pasty, about 3 minutes. Remove from the heat and cool, reserving ½ cup for the sauce.

Preheat the oven to 250°.

Divide the stuffing among the squash shells, put the tops back in place, and arrange in a roasting pan. Pour 1 cup of stock into the pan and bake for 1 hour. Turn off the oven, but keep the squashes in the warm oven while you make the sauce.

Pour the juices and browned bits from the roasting pan into a 10-inch nonstick skillet over high heat. Add the reserved stuffing, the remaining stock, the remaining sweet potatoes, and the remaining seasoning mix. Bring to a boil, whisking constantly, then whisk in the cream. Return just to a boil, then remove from the heat and purée in a blender or food processor. Serve each squash with a generous cup of the sauce.

Stuffed Potatoes with Lemon Grass and Greens and Sweet Coconut Milk and Lime Sauce

MAKES 8 SERVINGS

These beautiful potatoes are a good alternative to the usual cheese-stuffed twice-baked potatoes. If your market is out of mustard greens, you can use spinach; the substitution will make a huge difference, but the result will still be great. Lemon grass, which is often used in Thai cooking, contains citral, an essential oil also found in lemon peel, and that is the source of its astonishingly lemon-like flavor. If you can't find lemon grass, use lemon balm.

SEASONING MIX

1 tablespoon plus 1 teaspoon salt
2¾ teaspoons dried basil leaves
2¾ teaspoons dry mustard
2¾ teaspoons onion powder
2¾ teaspoons paprika
2¾ teaspoons ground dried árbol
chile peppers (see pages 1 and 2)

2 teaspoons ground cumin
1½ teaspoons cayenne
1½ teaspoons garlic powder
1½ teaspoons black pepper
1 teaspoon ground dried Anaheim
chile peppers (see pages 1 and 2)
¾ teaspoon white pepper

4 large white potatoes, each about
12 to 16 ounces
4 stalks lemon grass (see page 168)
4 tablespoons vegetable oil
1 cup chopped onions, about 1
small (5 ounces)
1 cup chopped celery, about 2
stalks
1 cup chopped red (or green) bell
peppers, about 1 medium

1 cup chopped yellow bell peppers,
about 1 medium
1 teaspoon minced fresh garlic,
about 1 clove
1 tablespoon minced fresh ginger
6 cups mustard greens, washed,
stems removed, and torn into
pieces
½ cup vegetable stock, preferred,
or chicken stock (see pages 5
and 6)

Preheat the oven to 425°.

Combine the seasoning mix ingredients in a small bowl and mix well.

Pierce the skin of each potato several times with the tines of a fork. Bake the potatoes until they are fully cooked, about 1 hour and 15 minutes. Cut the potatoes in half and carefully scoop out as much of the meat as possible while leaving the skins intact. Set aside the meat and the skins; you'll use 3 cups of the potato to stuff the skins, and 1½ cups of the potato in the sauce. If your potatoes are really large you'll have some left over for another use. Reduce the oven temperature to 350°.

Remove the leathery outer leaves from the lemon grass, cut up the fragrant inner stems, and chop them in a blender or pulverize them in a small coffee grinder. You want the lemon grass to be at least as small as ground coffee.

In a heavy 12-inch skillet over high heat, heat the oil just until it begins to smoke, about 3 to 4 minutes. Add the onions, celery, bell peppers, garlic, ginger, minced lemon grass, and 2 tablespoons of the seasoning mix. Reduce the heat to medium, cover and cook, uncovering to stir every 4 or 5 minutes, for 25 minutes. Carefully stir in the mustard greens and when they are thoroughly wilted, cover and cook for 12 minutes. Uncover and stir in the stock, 3 tablespoons plus 2½ teaspoons of the seasoning mix, and 3 cups of the potato meat. Cook uncovered, stirring every 3 or 4 minutes, for 10 minutes. Divide the stuffing evenly among the potato skins, place the stuffed skins in a baking pan, and bake until the skins are heated through, about 8 to 10 minutes. Serve hot with our Sweet Coconut Milk and Lime Sauce (recipe below).

Sweet Coconut Milk and Lime Sauce

MAKES 3 CUPS

2 tablespoons vegetable oil
½ cup chopped onions, about ½ small (2 ½ ounces)
½ cup chopped celery, about 1 stalk
¼ cup chopped green bell peppers, about ¼ medium
¼ cup chopped red bell peppers, about ¼ medium
¼ cup chopped yellow bell peppers, about ¼ medium

1½ cups baked white potatoes, about 1 medium
1 cup chicken stock (see pages 5 and 6)
¼ cup fresh lime juice
1 cup fresh orange juice
3 tablespoons dark brown sugar
1 (13-ounce) can unsweetened coconut milk (see page 166)
Zest of 1 lemon (see page 7)
Zest of 1 lime (see page 7)

In a 2-quart pot over high heat, heat the oil just until it begins to smoke, about 3 to 4 minutes. Add the onions, celery, bell peppers, and the remaining seasoning mix. Cook, stirring and scraping the pot every 2 minutes, until the vegetables are wilted and beginning to brown, about 8 minutes. Add the potatoes and continue to cook, stirring and scraping every 1 or 2 minutes, until the mixture is pasty and beginning to stick to the bottom of the pot, about 6 minutes. Stir in the stock, scrape the pan bottom completely, and bring to a boil. Add the lime juice, orange juice, and brown sugar. Return to a boil, stir well, reduce the heat to low, and simmer for 4 minutes. Stir in the coconut milk, bring just to a boil and reduce the heat to medium. Simmer for 10 minutes, then remove from the heat.

Purée the mixture in a food processor and return it to the pot. Bring the mixture to a boil, stir in the zest, and serve.

Cabbage and Rice

MAKES 8 OR 9 SIDE-DISH SERVINGS

The jasmine rice we call for has a very slightly sweet aroma and flavor, and works really well with cabbage. This great rice goes perfectly with any kind of meat, and I love it all by itself!

SEASONING MIX

2 teaspoons salt
1½ teaspoons ground cumin
1½ teaspoons onion powder
1¼ teaspoons dry mustard
1¼ teaspoons dried oregano leaves
1 teaspoon dried basil leaves

1 teaspoon garlic powder
1 teaspoon ground ginger
½ teaspoon cayenne
½ teaspoon black pepper
¼ teaspoon white pepper

2 tablespoons vegetable oil
4 packed cups cabbage, cut into
   julienne strips (looks like large
   coleslaw)

4 cups chicken stock or vegetable
   stock (see pages 5 and 6)
2 cups jasmine rice (see page 170)

Combine the seasoning mix ingredients in a small bowl and mix well.

Rinse the rice to remove the excess starch. Here's how to do it: place the uncooked rice in the bottom of a pot or large bowl, and fill with water. Rub the rice, a little at a time, between your hands. The water will become very cloudy or milky—that's the excess starch. Drain off the water, add clean water and repeat the rubbing process at least three more times. You'll see the water is much less milky, and now you're ready to proceed with this easy recipe.

In a heavy 4-quart pot over high heat, heat the oil just until it begins to smoke, about 3 to 4 minutes. Add the cabbage and the seasoning mix. Cook, stirring and scraping the pot every 3 to 4 minutes, until the mixture sticks hard, about 12 minutes, then stir in the stock and rice. Cover the pot, bring just to a boil, then reduce the heat to low and simmer until all the liquid is absorbed, about 20 minutes. Remove from the heat and let sit, covered, for 10 minutes. Stir gently before serving.

Choleta's Yucca Chips

Photograph No. 3

MAKES 4 TO 6 SERVINGS

Great with cold drinks or light meals, these crisp and spicy chips will probably disappear fast. If you do have any left over, they will stay fresh for several days in an airtight container—a plastic zipper bag works well—at room temperature. Choleta Pasia, whose husband, Chef Crispin Pasia, is one of my Test Kitchen assistants, loves these chips so much we just had to name them for her.

Yucca is extremely firm—you'll need a big, sharp knife to slice it, especially to get the super-thin slices for this recipe.

SEASONING MIX

1 tablespoon plus 2½ teaspoons sugar	½ teaspoon ground dried chipotle
¾ teaspoon salt	chile peppers (see pages 1 and 2)
¾ teaspoon cayenne	½ teaspoon ground cumin
¾ teaspoon garlic powder	½ teaspoon dry mustard
¾ teaspoon onion powder	¼ teaspoon white pepper

1 yucca root (see page 172), about 7 inches long	Vegetable oil for frying

Combine the seasoning mix ingredients in a small bowl and mix well.

Peel the yucca root and slice into very thin rounds, about 10 to the inch. You should have about 60 slices.

Heat enough oil to measure 2 inches deep in a large skillet to 350°. Use a cooking thermometer and adjust the heat so the temperature of the oil remains as steady as possible. An electric skillet, if you have one, works great. Fry the yucca slices, about 20 at a time, until they are golden brown, about 2 to 3 minutes. Drain on paper towels, and sprinkle evenly with the seasoning mix. Or place them in a plastic zipper bag along with the seasoning mix and shake gently until the chips are well coated—that's the easy way!

Deep-Fried Sweet Potato Chips

MAKES 4 SIDE-DISH SERVINGS

These chips are wonderful when they are just cooked, so serve them right away! And don't be misled by the name—they're just as great as a side dish served as you would serve sweet potatoes prepared any other way, as they are as a snack. Our Papaya Dipping Sauce (page 44) is wonderful with these chips.

SEASONING MIX

1 tablespoon sugar
2 teaspoons salt
1 teaspoon garlic powder
1 teaspoon dry mustard
1 teaspoon onion powder
1 teaspoon paprika

1 teaspoon ground dried Anaheim
    chile peppers (see pages 1 and 2)
1 teaspoon ground dried chipotle
    chile peppers (see pages 1 and 2)
½ teaspoon cayenne

1 sweet potato, about 7 inches long   Vegetable oil for frying

Combine the seasoning mix ingredients in a small bowl and mix well

Peel the sweet potato and slice it into 1/8-inch-thick rounds.

Pour enough oil to measure 2 inches deep into a large skillet and heat it to 350°. Use a cooking thermometer and adjust the heat to keep the oil as close to 350° as possible (it's really important to keep the oil at 350° so the chips will be nice and crisp). An electric skillet, if you have one, works great. Fry the sweet potato slices, in batches, until they are golden brown, about 3½ to 4 minutes. Drain on paper towels and sprinkle evenly with 2 teaspoons of the seasoning mix, or place the chips and seasoning mix in a plastic zipper bag and shake gently until the chips are evenly coated. Serve at once.

Save the remaining seasoning mix for another use.

STRICTLY

VEGETARIAN

Stuffed Mushrooms

MAKES 4 SERVINGS

These beautiful mushrooms, with their creamy sauce, are the perfect appetizer to get your dinner off to a dramatic and delicious start. It's very important to dice the vegetables into ¼-inch cubes so that they'll cook quickly but thoroughly. You want the carrots to retain their color, yet still be soft enough to mash and blend into the dressing. Don't mash them all, though, for a few intact little cubes add to the color and texture of the dish. You can use sweet potatoes, butternut squash, or any firm bright yellow or orange vegetable instead of the carrots. You'll notice that the sauce duplicates the flavor of the stuffing—it's a little different, like an echo. I love to do that!

SEASONING MIX

2 teaspoons salt
1 teaspoon dried basil leaves
1 teaspoon dill weed
1 teaspoon garlic powder
1 teaspoon ground ginger
1 teaspoon dry mustard

1 teaspoon onion powder
½ teaspoon cayenne
½ teaspoon ground cumin
½ teaspoon white pepper
¼ teaspoon ground nutmeg

12 (2-inch to 3-inch diameter) mushrooms for stuffing, stems removed
1 cup chopped pecans
2 tablespoons vegetable oil
1 cup onions, diced into ¼-inch cubes, about 1 small (5 ounces)
1 cup yellow bell peppers, diced into ¼-inch cubes, about 1 medium

2 cups carrots, diced into ¼-inch cubes
2 cups vegetable stock (see pages 5 and 6), in all
1½ cups mushrooms, diced into ¼-inch cubes
6 tablespoons all-purpose flour
Olive oil for coating
1 cup heavy cream

Combine the seasoning mix ingredients in a small bowl and mix well.

Season the mushroom caps evenly with 1 tablespoon plus 1 teaspoon of the seasoning mix.

In a small skillet over high heat, roast the pecans, stirring constantly to prevent burning, until they darken and give off a rich, nutty aroma, about 4 minutes. Remove from the skillet to stop the roasting and set aside.

In a heavy 10-inch skillet over high heat, heat the vegetable oil just until it begins to smoke, about 3 to 4 minutes. Add the onions, bell peppers, and carrots. Cover and cook, uncovering to stir every 1 or 2 minutes, until the vegetables start to wilt, about 5 minutes. Add 1 tablespoon of the seasoning mix and cook, stirring almost constantly, just until the vegetables start to brown, about 2 to 3 minutes. Add ½ cup stock and the remaining seasoning mix and cook, stirring almost constantly, for 2 minutes, then add the mushrooms and the flour. Stir and scrape the mixture until the flour is completely absorbed, about 2 minutes. Spread the mixture across the bottom of the skillet, and mash and scrape it up as it begins to stick to the bottom. Repeat this process until the mixture sticks hard, being sure to mix in the crust that forms on the bottom of the skillet. Stir in ½ cup stock and remove the skillet from the heat. Make the stuffing by combining 1 cup of the mixture with the roasted pecans (reserve the remaining mixture for the sauce).

Preheat the oven to 350°.

Brush the outside and inside of each mushroom cap with olive oil. Place the caps on a baking sheet. Shape 2 tablespoons of the stuffing into a ball and place it in one of the caps, shaping to fit. Fill the rest of the caps, and, if desired, brush the top of each stuffing ball with a little more olive oil. Bake them until the stuffing turns a rich golden brown and the mushroom caps are tender, about 20 minutes.

Meanwhile, make the sauce. Return the reserved mixture to the skillet over high heat and stir in ½ cup stock. Bring to a boil and stir in the cream and remaining stock. Return just to a boil, reduce the heat to low, and simmer for 4 minutes. Remove from the heat.

To serve, arrange 3 stuffed mushroom caps on each canapé plate and divide the sauce among the portions.

Butternut Squash and Spinach Lasagna

Photograph No. 13

MAKES 12 SERVINGS

This can be a totally vegetarian dish, but we offer the option of using chicken stock for those who really like that flavor. And it's so delicious that you'll never miss the meat! I know it looks complicated, but even though we've taken a lot of space to explain all the steps, there's nothing that's hard to do. You'll save time if you can manage four pots cooking at once: for the pasta, the squash and the greens fillings, and the sauce. If that sounds like too much the first time you prepare the recipe, don't worry, just do one or two at a time—it will all come out great in the end! If butternut squash isn't available, don't let that keep you from trying this great lasagna—substitute acorn squash, or even pumpkin!

SEASONING MIX

2 tablespoons light brown sugar
2 teaspoons dried oregano leaves
2 teaspoons salt
1½ teaspoons dill weed
1½ teaspoons onion powder
1½ teaspoons ground dried Anaheim
    chile peppers (see pages 1 and 2)

1 teaspoon dried basil leaves
1 teaspoon garlic powder
1 teaspoon paprika
1 teaspoon ground dried ancho chile
    peppers (see pages 1 and 2)
¾ teaspoon cayenne
½ teaspoon black pepper

1 pound dry lasagna noodles
9 tablespoons olive oil, in all
2 teaspoons salt
5½ cups chopped onions, about 3
    medium, in all
3½ cups chopped red bell peppers,
    about 3½ medium, in all
5 cups butternut squash, peeled and
    diced into ½-inch cubes
1 cup chopped celery, about 2 stalks
8 quarts fresh collard greens
    (loosely measured in a large
    container), stemmed and washed,
    about 3 bunches
6 quarts fresh spinach (loosely
    measured in a large container),

stemmed and washed, about 4
    bunches
½ cup heavy cream
4 tablespoons unsalted butter
1 (15-ounce) can tomato sauce, in all
2 (15-ounce) cans diced tomatoes
    (see page 7)
2 cups vegetable stock (see pages 5
    and 6)
4 ounces freshly grated Parmesan
    cheese
4 ounces freshly grated Romano
    cheese
1 pound ricotta cheese
10 ounces freshly grated provolone
    cheese

Combine the seasoning mix ingredients in a small bowl and mix well.

PASTA Cook the lasagna noodles in boiling water with 1 tablespoon of the olive oil and the salt until they reach the *al dente* stage. Check the noodle package for suggested amount of water and cooking time. Rinse in a colander under cold water, then drain and set aside.

SQUASH FILLING In a 4-quart pot over high heat, heat 2 table-spoons of the olive oil just until it begins to smoke, about 3 to 4 minutes. Add 1½ cups of the onions, 1½ cups of the red bell peppers, the butternut squash, and 2 tablespoons of the seasoning mix. Cook, stirring every 2 minutes, for 10 minutes, then remove from the heat and set aside.

GREENS FILLING In a 6-quart pot over high heat, heat 2 table-spoons of the olive oil just until it begins to smoke, about 3 to 4 minutes. Add 2 cups of the onions, the celery, and 2 tablespoons of the seasoning mix. Cook, stirring every 1 or 2 minutes, for 12 minutes. Add the collard greens, cover and cook, uncovering to stir every 4 or 5 minutes, for 20 minutes. Uncover and add the spinach, cream, and butter. Re-cover and cook, uncovering to stir every 1 or 2 minutes, for 15 minutes, then remove from the heat.

SAUCE In a heavy 2-quart pot over high heat, heat 2 tablespoons of the olive oil with the remaining 2 cups of onions, the remaining 2 cups of red bell peppers, and 2 tablespoons of the seasoning mix. Cook, stirring every 1 or 2 minutes, for 7 minutes. Add 1 cup of the tomato sauce and cook, stirring every 4 or 5 minutes, for 15 minutes. Stir in the remaining tomato sauce, the diced tomatoes, the remaining sea-soning mix, and the stock. Bring just to a boil, reduce the heat to medium, and simmer briskly for 25 minutes.

Preheat the oven to 350°.

ASSEMBLY Brush a 10-inch by 14-inch by 2½-inch pan with the remaining 2 tablespoons olive oil. Add a layer of one-third of the pasta, then a layer of all the greens, and a layer of all the squash. Sprinkle all the Parmesan and Romano cheeses over the squash, and add 2 cups of the sauce. Add another layer of one-third of the pasta, then spread on the ricotta cheese. Add 2 cups of the sauce and the remaining one-third of the pasta. Top with the remaining sauce and the provolone cheese.

Bake until the top is bubbly and golden brown, about 45 to 50 minutes. Let sit for 5 minutes before cutting into squares, so it will hold its shape and be easy to cut. Serve immediately.

Shiitake Mushrooms as a Main Course

MAKES 4 GENEROUS SERVINGS

If the only shiitake mushrooms available when you shop are smaller than the 2-inch diameter ones we specify, don't worry, just use more of them. Notice the aroma of the cardamom and coriander as you mix the seasonings, and I'll bet you'll agree that these spices add just the right exotic note to this vegetarian dish to lift it well above the ordinary.

SEASONING MIX

2 teaspoons salt
1½ teaspoons dried basil leaves
1½ teaspoons ground ginger
1½ teaspoons dry mustard
1½ teaspoons onion powder
1 teaspoon ground cardamom

1 teaspoon garlic powder
1 teaspoon paprika
¾ teaspoon ground coriander
½ teaspoon cayenne
½ teaspoon white pepper

6 tablespoons vegetable oil, in all
1 cup chopped onions, about 1 small (5 ounces)
½ cup chopped celery, about 1 stalk
3 cups shiitake mushrooms (see page 169), diced into ½-inch pieces, about 6 ounces
3 cups turnips, peeled and diced into ½-inch pieces, about 3 small (6 ounces each)
3 cups acorn squash, peeled and diced into ½-inch pieces

1 cup chopped red bell peppers, about 1 medium
2 cups unpeeled zucchini, diced into ½-inch pieces
3 cups vegetable stock (see pages 5 and 6), in all
3 tablespoons all-purpose flour, plus ½ cup for dredging
½ teaspoon salt
16 to 20 shiitake mushrooms, each about 2 inches in diameter, stems removed
4 cups cooked white rice, or brown rice, or your favorite pasta

Combine the seasoning mix ingredients in a small bowl and mix well.

In a heavy 4-quart pot over high heat, heat 2 tablespoons of the oil just until it begins to smoke, about 3 to 4 minutes. Add the onions, celery, diced shiitake mushrooms, and turnips. Cover and cook, uncovering to stir and scrape the bottom carefully every 3 or 4 minutes, for 10 minutes. Add the squash and bell peppers. Re-cover and cook for 4 minutes, then uncover and add the zucchini and 2 tablespoons of the seasoning mix. Stir very well, then add 1½ cups of stock. Stir well, then sprinkle 3 tablespoons flour on top of the mixture. Stir constantly until the flour is completely absorbed. (If necessary to absorb the flour, add ¼ cup more stock.) Cook, stirring 2 or 3 times, for 6 minutes, then stir in the remaining stock, 2 teaspoons of the seasoning mix, and the salt. Reduce the heat to very low, cover, and simmer for 10 minutes, then remove from heat.

Heat the remaining oil in a 10-inch skillet over high heat just until it begins to smoke, about 3 to 4 minutes.

Season the mushroom caps evenly with the remaining seasoning mix, dredge them in the remaining flour, and shake off the excess. *Immediately* transfer the seasoned, floured mushroom caps to the hot oil and cook them, turning once, until golden brown on both sides, about 3½ minutes in all.

Serve each person 1½ cups of the stew, accompanied by 4 mushroom caps and 1 cup of rice or pasta.

Eggplant with Vegetables in a Red Gravy

MAKES 4 SERVINGS

This is a vegetarian dish that feels like it has meat in it. It's great as a main course, or you could serve it as an appetizer, with one or two eggplant slices and ½ cup sauce per person. The provolone is a smoky white cheese, and gives the dish a hint of Italian flavor.

SEASONING MIX

2½ teaspoons salt
2 teaspoons dried basil leaves
2 teaspoons onion powder
1¼ teaspoons garlic powder
1¼ teaspoons dry mustard
1¼ teaspoons dried oregano leaves
1¼ teaspoons paprika

1¼ teaspoons ground dried New
    Mexico chile peppers (see pages 1
    and 2)
1 teaspoon cayenne
¾ teaspoon black pepper
¾ teaspoon ground dried guajillo
    chile peppers (see pages 1 and 2)
¾ teaspoon ground savory

3 tablespoons olive oil

1 cup chopped onions, about 1 small (5 ounces)

1 cup chopped celery, about 2 stalks

3 cups unpeeled eggplant, diced into ½-inch cubes, about 1 small (11 or 12 ounces)

3 cups peeled yucca (see page 172), diced into ½-inch cubes

1 cup chopped red bell peppers, about 1 medium

1 cup chopped yellow bell peppers, about 1 medium

1 (15-ounce) can diced tomatoes (see page 7)

1 (15-ounce) can tomato sauce

2 teaspoons minced fresh garlic, about 2 cloves

1 teaspoon minced fresh ginger

2 cups vegetable stock (see pages 5 and 6)

8 ounces thinly sliced provolone cheese

16 slices unpeeled Japanese eggplant, each about 3/8-inch thick, cut diagonally about 2 inches by 6 inches each, 3 or 4 eggplants, depending upon size

Combine the seasoning mix ingredients in a small bowl and mix well.

In a heavy 4-quart pot or 12-inch skillet over high heat, heat the oil just until it begins to smoke, about 3 to 4 minutes. Add the onions and celery and cook, stirring every 1 or 2 minutes, for 5 minutes, then add the diced eggplant and yucca. Cook, stirring and scraping the pot every 1 or 2 minutes, for 4 minutes. Add the bell peppers and cook, stirring and scraping almost constantly, for 5 minutes, then add 1 tablespoon plus 1 teaspoon of the seasoning mix. Cook, stirring and scraping the pot constantly, for 2 minutes, then add the diced tomatoes. Cook for 4 minutes, then stir in the tomato sauce, garlic, and ginger. Cook, stirring and scraping constantly, for 3 minutes, then add the stock. Bring just to a boil, reduce the heat to low and simmer, stirring and scraping the bottom of the pot every 4 or 5 minutes, for 20 minutes. Remove from the heat.

While the sauce is cooking, sprinkle the sliced eggplant evenly with 2 tablespoons of the seasoning mix and gently pat it in.

Preheat the oven to 250°.

Preheat a heavy nonstick 12-inch skillet over high heat to 350°, about 3 minutes. An electric skillet, if it can be heated empty (check the owner's manual) works perfectly. Add the eggplant slices and cook, turning once or twice, until golden brown, about 3 minutes. Transfer the eggplant to a baking sheet and top evenly with the provolone cheese slices. Place in the oven just until the cheese melts, about 3 to 5 minutes. For each serving, fan 4 slices of the eggplant over 2 cups of the tomato/eggplant mixture. This is one of my favorite dishes in the book because it's so satisfying.

Candied Belgian Endive

MAKES 6 SERVINGS

This unique dish can be served as a dynamite appetizer or as a side dish to accompany broiled fish, chicken or pork chops.

Someone asked me how I came up with this recipe, as it's so different from anything I've done before. Well, every once in a while you get an unusual idea, you try it, and it works. This was one of those times.

SEASONING MIX

1 teaspoon ground ginger
1 teaspoon ground dried guajillo
   chile peppers (see pages 1 and 2)
1 teaspoon salt

¾ teaspoon ground cinnamon
½ teaspoon dry mustard
½ teaspoon ground nutmeg

12 Belgian endives, cut in half
   lengthwise
½ pound (2 sticks) unsalted butter
½ medium-size unpeeled lemon,
   cut into 12 thin slices, seeds
   removed

½ medium-size unpeeled orange,
   cut into 12 thin slices, seeds
   removed
1½ cups sugar
1 cup vegetable stock (see pages 5
   and 6)

Combine the seasoning mix ingredients in a small bowl and mix well.

Preheat the oven to 325°.

In a large baking pan, arrange the endive halves, cut side up.

In a heavy 10- or 12-inch skillet over medium-high heat, melt the butter, and as it melts stir in the seasoning mix, then arrange the lemon and orange slices in a thin layer on the bottom of the skillet. When the butter is completely melted, add the sugar and stock. Whisk gently, enjoying the spicy aroma, until the sugar dissolves. Bring the mixture to a boil, stirring frequently, and cook until all the sugar is thoroughly melted, about 4 to 5 minutes. Remove from the heat and pour evenly over the endive halves.

Bake until the endive halves are cooked through, about 1 hour to 1 hour and 15 minutes. Serve each portion with 1 tablespoon of the delicious liquid and a lemon slice and an orange slice for garnish.

Sautéed Zucchini with Vegetable Cream Pasta

MAKES 4 SERVINGS

This is a hearty dish, with three kinds of squash, plenty of pasta in every portion, the richness of cream and sour cream, and the wonderful smoky flavor of roasted garlic. We've listed three colors of bell peppers, but the yellow and red ones can be extremely expensive, so use 1½ cups of green ones if you like. You'll notice there's a good bit of paprika, which adds a great color and sweet pepper taste. It's made by grinding the pods of sweet red peppers, and the color can range from bright red-orange to a deep blood-red. Most commercial paprika sold in this country comes from Spain, South America, Hungary, and California, and its flavor can range from mild to pungent and HOT. Unfortunately paprika can go bad and still be a beautiful color, so be sure to taste your supply before you begin the recipe. If it tastes bitter, discard it and open a new jar.

SEASONING MIX

1½ teaspoons salt
1¼ teaspoons paprika
1 teaspoon ground ginger
¾ teaspoon dried basil leaves
¾ teaspoon dill weed
¾ teaspoon garlic powder
¾ teaspoon onion powder

¾ teaspoon oregano leaves
¾ teaspoon ground dried Anaheim
  chile peppers (see pages 1 and 2)
½ teaspoon ground cumin
½ teaspoon black pepper
¼ teaspoon cayenne
¼ teaspoon white pepper

2 large unpeeled zucchini, cut
  diagonally into 16 slices, each
  about 2 inches by 5 inches
1 cup heavy cream
½ cup sour cream (see page 3)
3 tablespoons vegetable oil
½ cup chopped green bell peppers,
  about ½ medium
½ cup chopped red bell peppers,
  about ½ medium
½ cup chopped yellow bell
  peppers, about ½ medium
½ cup chopped fresh Anaheim
  chile peppers (see pages 1 and 2)

½ cup chopped fresh banana
  peppers (see pages 1 and 2)
1 bulb roasted garlic (see page 4),
  chopped, about 6 tablespoons
1 cup butternut squash, peeled
  and diced into ½-inch cubes
3 cups unpeeled zucchini, diced
  into ½-inch cubes
3 cups white squash (or whatever
  squashes are available), peeled
  and diced into ½-inch cubes
2 teaspoons minced fresh ginger
3 cups your favorite cooked pasta

Combine the seasoning mix ingredients in a small bowl and mix well.

Sprinkle the zucchini slices evenly with 1 tablespoon plus 2 teaspoons of the seasoning mix and gently pat it in.

In a small bowl stir together the heavy cream and sour cream just until blended.

In a heavy 4-quart pot over high heat, heat the oil just until it begins to smoke, about 3 to 4 minutes. Add the five peppers, the roasted garlic, and the butternut squash and cook, stirring occasionally at first, then almost constantly toward the end of the cooking time, for 8 minutes. *The smallest pieces of the peppers will get really dark really fast during this time, but don't worry—keep stirring (and reduce the heat if you absolutely must) because you're bringing out the peppers' natural sweetness as you caramelize them.* Add the diced zucchini, white (or other) squash, and the remaining seasoning mix. Cook, stirring every 2 to 3 minutes, for 10 minutes, then add the ginger. Stir well for 3 minutes, then reduce the heat to medium (if you didn't do so earlier). Add the heavy cream and sour cream and stir until the mixture is well blended, about 3 to 4 minutes. Remove from the heat.

Preheat a heavy nonstick 10-inch skillet over medium-high heat until hot, about 3 minutes. Sauté the seasoned zucchini slices in the dry skillet for 4 to 5 minutes, turning once, until they are moderately brown on both sides. Add the pasta to the sauce, stir until it is thoroughly heated, and serve. For each portion, serve 4 zucchini slices with 2 cups of the pasta and sauce.

If you want to make a really pretty presentation, you can fan out the zucchini slices on top of the pasta and cream.

The Three Cs—Charyn, Cherriepin and Cherrielet—

Tricolor Vegetable Terrine with Roasted Pepper Sauce

Photograph No. 14

MAKES 4 MAIN-COURSE OR 8 APPETIZER SERVINGS

The three Cs for whom this dish is named are the charming daughters of Chef Crispin Pasia, who created the recipe.

This delicious terrine is a very dramatic dish to set before your guests, and will make your reputation as an innovative host. A simple way to cook the three colors of vegetables and save the cooking liquid is to use a metal colander inside the pot—you can easily lift it out with tongs, hold it over the pot for a moment to drain the vegetables, then empty them out and put it back in for the next step. The leeks are so large you won't need the colander—you can remove them from the cooking liquid with tongs or a slotted spoon.

You can make the wonderful sauce any time, using whatever stock you have on hand and seasoning it to your taste, and use it to sauce fish cakes, meat patties, or any aspic. You also can vary the colors in the terrine according to the season, using vegetables whose colors are appropriate to the closest holiday. Take the idea and run with it!

SEASONING MIX

2¼ teaspoons salt
1 teaspoon ground cinnamon
¾ teaspoon dried basil leaves
¾ teaspoon garlic powder
¾ teaspoon onion powder
¾ teaspoon dried oregano leaves

¾ teaspoon dried thyme leaves
½ teaspoon cayenne
½ teaspoon ground nutmeg
½ teaspoon black pepper
½ teaspoon white pepper

4 quarts vegetable stock (see pages 5 and 6) or water
3 whole leeks, washed and bottoms removed
3 cups white potatoes, peeled and diced into ½-inch cubes, about 2 medium (10 ounces each)
2 cups chopped onions, about 2 small (5 ounces each) in all
1 cup heavy cream, in all

7 (7-gram) packages gelatin, in all
3 cups carrots, diced into ½-inch pieces
½ pound fresh collard greens, washed, stemmed, and torn into 3-inch pieces
½ pound fresh spinach, washed, stemmed, and torn into 3-inch pieces

Combine the seasoning mix ingredients in a small bowl and mix well.

Place an 8-quart pot over high heat and add the stock or water and 2 tablespoons of the seasoning mix. Bring to a boil, about 20 minutes, add the leeks, and boil until they are tender, about 10 to 12 minutes. Remove the leeks and set them aside, saving the liquid. Return the liquid to a boil, and repeat the cooking process, returning the liquid to a boil each time, with the other vegetables as follows:

potatoes and ½ cup onions—until tender, about 12 minutes

carrots and ½ cup onions—until tender, about 20 minutes

collard greens and 1 cup of the onions—until tender, about 8 minutes, then add the spinach and cook for 5 minutes longer

Reserve 1 cup of the cooking liquid for the sauce and discard the remainder.

When the leeks are cool enough to handle, cut off the dark green leaves, leaving the white parts and about 2 inches of the light green part. Peel the individual leaves, which will be in long strips, and drain them on paper towels. Set aside.

Make each of the layers—the white potato purée, the orange carrot purée, and the green greens purée—separately, but the same way: whisk 2 packets (3 packets for the greens) of the gelatin into ½ cup hot water until it is dissolved. Combine each of the vegetables, in turn, in a food processor or blender with the dissolved gelatin, ¼ cup of the cream (½ cup for the greens), and 1 teaspoon of the seasoning mix. Process until the mixture is puréed, set aside, and clean the appliance for the next purée.

Line a terrine mold or an 8½-inch by 4½-inch by 2½-inch loaf pan with plastic wrap, allowing it to hang out about 3 inches, then with pieces of the leek, allowing the ends of the leek strips to hang out about 1½ inches over the edge of the mold in all directions. Be sure that the inside of the mold is covered completely.

Spread 1½ cups of the potato mixture over the bottom of the mold, then spread 1½ cups of the carrot purée evenly on top of the potato layer, and spread 1½ cups of the greens purée evenly on top of the carrot layer. Cover the top with more strips of leek, then fold the overhanging strips of leek back onto the center. Fold the excess plastic wrap over the top of the mold. Refrigerate until firmly set, preferably overnight, but at least 6 hours.

To serve, carefully turn the terrine out of the mold onto a platter. If it doesn't loosen easily, either rub the outside of the mold with a hot towel before removing the mold, or return the mold to right-side-up position and very briefly dip it into hot water, quickly dry the mold, and try again. Cut into 1-inch-thick slices. Surround each slice with 2 tablespoons of the sauce (recipe below). Or, if you want to make a dramatic presentation like those you see in cuisine magazines or at upscale restaurants, drizzle a little of the sauce in a pattern on the plate, then place the terrine slice on top of the sauce. You can leave each slice whole, or you can cut it diagonally into four triangles, then arrange the triangles up-ended, so that they form an "x" when viewed from above. Talk about impressive!

Roasted Pepper Sauce

1 tablespoon vegetable oil
½ cup chopped onions
1 cup chopped roasted red bell
  peppers (see page 4)
¼ cup chopped roasted fresh
  Anaheim chile peppers (see
  pages 1 and 2)

2 tablespoons chopped roasted
  fresh jalapeño chile peppers (see
  pages 1 and 2)
1 teaspoon minced fresh garlic
2 tablespoons unsalted butter
1 tablespoon dark brown sugar

In a 10-inch skillet over high heat, heat the oil just until it begins to smoke, about 3 to 4 minutes. Add the onions, red bell peppers, and the Anaheim peppers and cook, stirring almost constantly, for 4 minutes. Add the cup of reserved cooking liquid from the vegetables and bring to a boil. Add the jalapeños and garlic, and stir well. Remove from the heat and purée in a food processor or blender. Return the purée to the skillet and bring almost to a boil, then whisk in the butter and brown sugar. Remove from the heat.

DESTINATION:

DESSERTS!

Stir-Fried Rice Pudding

MAKES 9 SERVINGS

At refrigerator temperature this wonderful pudding loses all its distinctive, delicious taste, so follow our suggestion and serve it at room temperature or slightly warm. It's unusual to have chile peppers in a dessert, but don't be put off—try it once, and I'll bet you'll love it!

SEASONING MIX

3 tablespoons sugar
3 tablespoons light brown sugar
1 teaspoon Chinese 5-spice powder
    (see page 166)
1 teaspoon ground cinnamon
1 teaspoon ground nutmeg

1 teaspoon paprika
1 teaspoon ground dried New Mexico
    chile peppers (see pages 1 and 2)
1 teaspoon ground dried pasilla chile
    peppers (see pages 1 and 2)
1 teaspoon salt

2 cups Converted® rice
1 small fresh pineapple, peeled,
    cored, and sliced into 5 rings,
    each about ¾-inch thick, about 1
    pound
1½ cups fresh cherries, pitted
½ teaspoon salt
Juice of 2 medium-size oranges,
    about 1¼ pounds total weight,
    about 1 cup juice
Juice of 2 medium-size limes,
    about ½ pound total weight,
    about ¼ cup juice

1 (14-ounce) can sweetened
    condensed milk
1 (13½-ounce) can unsweetened
    coconut milk (see page 166)
4 tablespoons unsalted butter, in
    all
½ cup dried currants
¼ cup vegetable oil
½ cup pecans, toasted (see page 7),
    then broken into small pieces

Combine the seasoning mix ingredients in a small bowl and mix well.

Place the pineapple rings on a flat surface, sprinkle the top sides evenly with a total of 1 tablespoon of the seasoning mix, and gently pat the seasonings in. Turn the rings over, sprinkle these sides evenly with 1 tablespoon of the seasoning mix, and pat it in.

Reserve 8 of the cherries and leave them whole for decoration. Cut the rest of the cherries into 4 pieces each and set them aside.

In a 4-quart saucepan, bring 1 quart of water to a boil over high heat. Add the rice and return just to a boil, then reduce the heat to low.

Cover and simmer until the water is absorbed and the rice is done, about 20 minutes. Remove from the heat and set aside to cool.

Meanwhile, combine the orange and lime juices with the condensed milk and coconut milk.

In a 12-inch nonstick skillet over high heat, melt 2 tablespoons of the butter. As soon as it begins to sizzle, add the seasoned pineapple rings to the skillet. Cook, turning every 2 minutes, until the rings are light golden brown, about 8 minutes in all. Remove the pineapple rings and make the sauce by adding the juice/milk mixture to the skillet. Whisk to dissolve the remaining seasoning mix in the skillet, bring the sauce just to a boil, then stir in the currants. Return to a rolling boil, then turn off heat and whisk in the remaining 2 tablespoons butter and the remaining seasoning mix. Set the sauce aside.

Reserve 2 of the pineapple slices for garnish. Shred the rest of the slices with a knife and fork—hold each slice in turn with the knife and tear it apart with the fork. Set all the shredded pineapple aside.

Heat a wok or a 12-inch skillet with high sides over high heat until it is extremely hot (500°), about 10 minutes. It's very important to get the pan really, really hot, so the rice won't stick. Also, this very high heat changes the flavor of the rice, and a lower heat just won't make it! Add the oil, and when it smokes, add the cooked rice, cherry pieces, shredded pineapple, and pecans. Fry, stirring constantly, just until the rice turns light tan, about 4 minutes. Place the rice mixture in a 3-quart casserole dish. Pour the sauce over the top, and decorate the top with the reserved 8 cherries and 2 pineapple slices. Serve warm or at room temperature, and refrigerate any leftover pudding.

Pasia's Ricotta Pie

MAKES 6 SERVINGS

This may remind you a little bit of a cheesecake, but instead of a crumb crust, we've used light and flaky phyllo dough. And we've jazzed up the filling with orange liqueur, currants, pecans, and butterscotch chips! The rich, creamy result is fit for royalty, yet there's nothing difficult about the recipe, so it's never been easier to show off your culinary skills.

½ cup plus 2 tablespoons sugar, in all

3 tablespoons ground blanched almonds

6 tablespoons all-purpose flour

1½ cups half-and-half cream

Zest (see page 7) of 3 medium-size oranges, about ¼ cup

4 large eggs

1 (15-ounce) container ricotta cheese, soft variety, about 1¾ cups

6 tablespoons sour cream

2 teaspoons vanilla

¼ cup Grand Marnier® or your favorite orange-flavored liqueur

½ cup dried currants

6 ounces butterscotch chips

¼ cup raisins

½ cup chopped toasted pecans (see page 7)

4 tablespoons unsalted butter, melted and cooled

6 sheets phyllo dough (see page 170), each about 14 inches by 18 inches

Combine ½ cup of the sugar, the almonds, and the flour, and sift together.

Place the half-and-half cream in a 12-inch nonstick skillet over high heat and whisk in the almond/flour mixture. Bring to a boil, whisking constantly—as soon as it reaches a boil it will begin to thicken. Reduce the heat to low and cook, whisking constantly, for 5 minutes, then remove from the heat. Pour the mixture onto a sheet pan and chill in the refrigerator until the temperature of the mixture is lowered to 50°.

Place ½ cup of water in an 8-inch nonstick skillet over high heat and add the remaining 2 tablespoons sugar and the orange zest. Bring just to a boil, then remove from the heat. Strain out the orange zest and mince it.

In a mixer fitted with a whisk attachment whisk the eggs for 3 minutes, then add the ricotta. Continue to whisk for 2 minutes, then add the chilled mixture, the orange zest, sour cream, vanilla and Grand Marnier. Continue to whip on the lowest speed until the mixture is smooth, about 5 minutes. Add the currants, butterscotch chips, raisins and roasted pecans.

Preheat the oven to 300°.

If you've never worked with phyllo pastry before, read the package directions. Don't let it intimidate you, but do handle it with great care, as it tears very easily. Assemble the phyllo pastry by laying 1 sheet of the dough on a clean, dry work surface. Brush the top of the sheet lightly with butter. Lay another sheet of phyllo on top of the buttered sheet and repeat the process until you have 3 buttered layers. When you have 3 layers, carefully line an 8-inch by 8-inch cake pan with the buttered sheets, allowing the edges of the dough to hang over the sides. Gently blot up any excess butter with a paper towel. Make another 3 layers of buttered phyllo sheets as above and place them in the pan at right angles to the previous 3 sheets. Place the ricotta mixture in the pan and gently even it out. With scissors trim the excess phyllo dough, leaving about ½ inch hanging over the sides. Fold this remaining border toward the center of the pan so that it is angled inward but not touching the filling.

Bake until the edges of the phyllo crust are lightly browned, about 1 hour. Cool at least 4 hours before serving or, if you prefer, refrigerate the pie and serve it cold. It's wonderful either way.

First Fried Cookies

Fried cookies or sweet fritters, who cares what you call them as long as you have plenty for everyone! Crispy and golden brown on the outside, tender and touched with nuts and fresh fruit on the inside, they lure anyone within sniffing range with their wonderful aroma. They're ridiculously easy to prepare, but be sure to keep the batter very cold until each cookie is fried. And enjoy them while they're hot, for like most fried foods they're best if eaten as soon as they're cool enough to handle. You can use any fruit that is fresh and tempting at the market—if you don't mind pitting them, fresh cherries would taste great and echo the flavor of the kirschwasser.

¼ cup chopped pecans
¼ cup chopped walnuts
¼ cup chopped hazelnuts
3 large eggs
1 teaspoon cream of tartar
6 tablespoons sugar
3 tablespoons dark rum
3 tablespoons kirschwasser (see page 168)
1 teaspoon vanilla extract
¼ teaspoon ground cinnamon
½ teaspoon paprika

¼ teaspoon ground dried chipotle chile peppers (see pages 1 and 2)
¼ teaspoon salt
2 teaspoons baking soda
¾ cup all-purpose flour
¾ cup corn flour (see page 167)
¾ cup water
¼ cup sliced fresh strawberries, cherries, or other fresh fruit, plus
¼ cup fresh blueberries
Vegetable oil for frying
Powdered sugar, optional

Preheat the oven to 300°.

Toast the pecans and walnuts in a dry cake pan or pie pan in the oven until they begin to darken and give off a rich toasted aroma, about 20 to 25 minutes. Toast the hazelnuts in a separate pan also in the oven until the brown skins rub off evenly, about 30 to 35 minutes. Remove from the oven and cool slightly, then rub the hazelnuts together in a kitchen towel or between your fingers to remove the skins. Set aside.

Separate the eggs. In the small bowl of an electric mixer with a whisk attachment, beat the whites and the cream of tartar until they form stiff peaks, about 4 minutes.

In the large bowl of the mixer combine the yolks, sugar, rum, kirschwasser, vanilla, cinnamon, paprika. chipotle, salt, baking soda, all-purpose flour, and the corn flour. Mix just until combined, then add the water and beat until the batter is well combined and smooth, about 2 minutes. Gently stir in the nuts, strawberries (or other fruit), and blueberries, then very gently fold in the egg whites. Refrigerate the batter until very cold, at least 1 hour.

When the batter is very cold, pour enough oil into a 12-inch skillet to measure 1 inch deep and heat it over medium heat to 300°. Use an electric skillet or a cooking thermometer and adjust the heat to keep the oil temperature between of 300° and 325°. When the oil reaches the correct temperature, remove the batter from the refrigerator and place it in a large bowl one-third full of ice and water. *It is very important to keep the batter very cold, for it is extremely delicate and will dissipate in the hot oil if it warms while sitting out.* With a large serving spoon, scoop up about 3 tablespoons of the batter and gently drop it into the oil, moving the spoon sideways to drag the batter into an elongated oval shape. Fry the "cookie," turning every 30 seconds or so, until it is medium brown and crispy, about 2 to 3 minutes. When the cookie is done remove it from the oil and place it on paper towels to drain. Gently stir as you scoop up the batter for the next cookie (to keep it from separating), and repeat the process until all the batter is used. Sprinkle the cookies with powdered sugar if you like, and serve immediately.

Chocolate Crêpes
with Pecan-Banana Sauce

MAKES 8 SERVINGS

Luscious and rich with heavy cream, chocolate, and pecans, this is not a dessert to serve every day. But for those who long for something sinfully delicious once in a while, here is a treat that will satisfy their craving. Two cautions are in order, though. One is to be sure your stove is level, or you'll have a hard time keeping the crêpes round and even. The other thing is to plan to make this dessert when your kitchen will be cool—in a warm kitchen the stacks are likely to slip before you finish them and get them into the refrigerator. If you have baking or roasting or a lot of steamy stove-top cooking to do, make the dessert ahead of time.

CRÊPES

¾ cup all-purpose flour
¼ cup buckwheat flour (see page 165)
4 tablespoons unsweetened cocoa powder
3 tablespoons sugar

½ teaspoon baking powder
¼ teaspoon salt
2 cups milk
2 tablespoons vegetable oil
3 large eggs, lightly beaten

SAUCE

6 tablespoons unsalted butter
1½ cups dark brown sugar
1 teaspoon ground cinnamon
½ teaspoon ground nutmeg
1 tablespoon vanilla
1 cup heavy cream
2 ounces butterscotch chips

4 medium-size bananas, peeled and sliced, about 3 cups (use bananas that still have a little green on the tips)
1½ cups toasted pecans (see page 7)
¼ cup Kahlua®

3 cups heavy cream

MAKE THE CRÊPES Combine the all-purpose flour, buckwheat flour, cocoa, sugar, baking powder, and salt in the bowl of an electric mixer with a whisk or paddle attachment. Whisk at low speed just until the ingredients are combined, about 1 minute. Add the milk, oil, and eggs and whisk until the batter is well combined, about 5 minutes.

Preheat an 8-inch nonstick skillet over medium heat for 4 minutes. Pour ¼ cup of the batter into the skillet, tilting the skillet to distribute the batter evenly and allowing it to come slightly up the sides of the pan. Cook until the edges of the crêpe become slightly crisp, about 2 minutes, then with a plastic spatula or your fingers, turn the crêpe over and cook for 1 minute. Transfer the cooked crêpe to a sheet pan (it's OK to stack them) and set aside. Repeat the process, wiping or scraping the spatula clean between uses, until all the crêpes are cooked—you should have enough batter to make 12 crêpes.

MAKE THE SAUCE In a 12-inch nonstick skillet over high heat, combine the butter, brown sugar, cinnamon, nutmeg, and vanilla. Whisk constantly until the butter melts and combines with the brown sugar, then whisk in the cream. Bring to a boil, whisking constantly to avoid burning, then reduce the heat to medium and add the butterscotch chips. Whisk until the chips melt, then reduce the heat to low, add the bananas and stir gently for 2 minutes. Remove from the heat and stir in the toasted pecans and Kahlua. Set aside to cool.

ASSEMBLY Whip the cream in an electric mixer at medium-high speed until it forms stiff peaks. Place the whipped cream in a pastry bag fitted with a medium-size star tip.

Place 1 crêpe on a large serving plate. Pipe a circle of whipped cream around the edge of the crêpe and spread ¼ cup of the sauce inside the whipped cream circle. Top with another crêpe and repeat the process until you have 6 layers. Repeat the entire process to create another 6-layer stack. Cut each stack into 4 quarters to make 8 desserts. Serve each quarter on a dessert plate and garnish with a rosette of whipped cream, if desired.

White Chocolate and Cheese Custard with Berry Sauce

Photograph No. 15

MAKES 16 SERVINGS

Smooth and rich, this is a dessert for times when you want to pull out all the stops and dazzle your guests, yet it couldn't be simpler to prepare. I like it so much, I made it even after we'd finished the television segment, and decided to try a fresh berry sauce with it. It's great! You can use any fresh berries in the sauce, and you might add a few more as garnish. A helpful hint: chopping will be a lot easier if the chocolate, knife, and cutting surface are cool. If your kitchen is very warm, refrigerate the chocolate, knife, and a cutting board for a while first. Notice that we specify soft goat cheese—it's important to use soft cheese to get the right texture for this great dessert.

CUSTARD

1 cup all-purpose flour
½ cup sugar
1 cup milk
1 teaspoon vanilla
3 large eggs
1 (8-ounce) container sour cream
3½ ounces mild soft goat cheese, such as Montrachet®

5½ ounces sharp soft goat cheese, such as Silver Goat®
2 tablespoons unsalted butter, melted and cooled
14 ounces good quality white chocolate (see page 172), such as Lindt®, Tobler®, or Ghiradelli®), chopped into small pieces

Preheat the oven to 350°.

In the bowl of an electric mixer with a whisk or paddle attachment, combine the flour, sugar, milk, and vanilla. Beat at low speed for 1 minute to combine. Add the eggs and sour cream, increase the speed to medium-low and beat until they are combined. Add the goat cheeses and beat until they are combined, about 2 minutes.

Brush the melted butter evenly over the inside a 2-quart casserole dish or baking pan, or small ramekins, sprinkle the white chocolate evenly over the bottom(s), then pour in the beaten mixture. Place this dish (or pan or ramekins) in a larger pan and fill the larger pan with enough water to come halfway up the sides of the inner dish (or pan or ramekins). Bake until the surface appears firm and a knife inserted into the custard comes out clean, about 50 minutes.

When the custard is done, remove from the oven and invert onto a serving platter. Should any of the chocolate stick to the baking pan, simply scrape it out and put it on top of the custard. If you baked your custard in a pan, cut it into squares, and if you baked the custard in ramekins, you can serve it in them. Serve with the Berry Sauce (recipe below).

Berry Sauce

2 pints fresh berries

½ cup sugar, or to taste

While the custard is baking, make the sauce by puréeing the berries and sugar in a blender or food processor until smooth.

Stilton Cheese and Sweet Potato Pudding

MAKES 6 SERVINGS

It's important to buy a really good quality Stilton cheese, one that's not cloudy. Generally, the more blue there is in it, the better it is. I think the taste of Stilton works great with sweet potatoes. People asked how I came up with the combination, especially for a dessert. It started when I was enjoying some really wonderful Stilton cheese. Out of the blue the taste of sweet potatoes intruded and it occurred to me that they might go together. Sure enough when I tried it, it was wonderful. It's different, but I think one of the great things about cooking is coming up with new taste sensations. By the way, the cheese will crumble easily if it's cold—don't remove it from the refrigerator until you're ready to use it.

8 medium-size to small sweet potatoes, about 3 pounds total, scrubbed	1 stick unsalted butter, melted 1 (8-ounce) container unflavored low-fat yogurt (see page 3)
½ teaspoon salt	3 large eggs
3 tablespoons dark brown sugar	5 ounces Stilton cheese, crumbled

Preheat the oven to 350°.

Bake the potatoes until they are soft inside, about 45 minutes to 1 hour. As soon as they are cool enough to handle, peel the potatoes—you should have about 3 cups—and place them in an electric mixer with a whip attachment, along with the salt and brown sugar. Whip the potatoes at medium speed and when the mixture is smooth, about 2 minutes, add the melted butter. Continue to whip until the butter is incorporated, then add the yogurt and the eggs. Beat at high speed until the color lightens and the mixture becomes light and fluffy, about 5 minutes.

Pour the potato mixture to a 9-inch by 13-inch casserole dish or baking pan, or to 6 individual ramekins, then shove bits of the Stilton cheese into the mix at random places. Place the pan or dishes in another pan large enough to hold them. Pour enough water into the larger pan to come about 2/3 the way up the sides of the casserole dish or ramekins, and bake until the cheese bits are melted and the top is just beginning to brown, about 45 minutes. Serve hot or let cool to room temperature, but don't serve it cold. If you refrigerate the pudding, warm it slightly before serving.

Cane Syrup Coconut Cake

MAKES 16 SERVINGS

This dense, tasty cake smells and tastes a little like gingerbread, because the cane syrup we use is a first cousin of molasses, but that's as far as the relationship goes. The coconut sauce is an original, and is so good that you're going to enjoy pouring it over other fruit and desserts. Imagine grilled orange slices, sprinkled with just a touch of cinnamon, and topped with the sauce—easy and delicious! Please notice that the amount of coconut milk called for in the cake is 1 cup, not one can. You'll have 5½ fluid ounces left over for another recipe or to add great flavor to a sauce or gravy.

CAKE

4 tablespoons unsalted butter, softened

¼ cup sugar

2 large eggs

½ teaspoon vanilla

½ cup cane syrup (see page 165)

1½ cups all-purpose flour

½ teaspoon baking soda

2 teaspoons baking powder

¼ teaspoon salt

1 cup unsweetened coconut milk (see page 166)

Vegetable oil cooking spray

COCONUT SAUCE

1 (13½-ounce) can unsweetened coconut milk (see page 166)

½ cup heavy cream

2 tablespoons cane syrup (see page 165)

½ cup shredded sweetened coconut, a moist variety such as Baker's®

2 tablespoons unsalted butter

TOPPING

2 cups mixed ripe fresh fruit, such as blueberries, blackberries, strawberry pieces, small slices of plum, peach, or banana

MAKE THE CAKE Preheat the oven to 350°.

In the bowl of an electric mixer with a paddle attachment, cream the butter and sugar at low speed until light and lemon-colored. Blend in the eggs one at a time, mixing well after each addition, then blend in the vanilla and syrup. With the mixer still on low speed, add the flour, soda, baking powder, and salt, and beat until well combined, then stir in the coconut milk. As soon as all the ingredients are blended, increase the speed to medium-fast (#5) and beat for 8 minutes, scraping the sides of the bowl with a rubber spatula every minute or so.

Lightly coat an 8-inch by 8-inch baking pan with vegetable oil cooking spray, and pour in the cake batter. Bake until the surface looks firm and a knife inserted into the center comes out clean, about 40 to 45 minutes. Invert the cake onto a flat surface and set it aside to cool. When it reaches room temperature, cut it into 2-inch square pieces.

MAKE THE SAUCE Pour the coconut milk and cream into a 4-quart pot and place it over high heat. Whisking constantly, bring the mixture to a boil. When the milk begins to boil it will spatter very violently, like a white volcano. Immediately reduce the heat to low and simmer, stirring constantly, until the spattering subsides. Continue to cook, stirring every 2 minutes at first, then almost constantly toward the end of the cooking time, until the mixture is bubbling heavily again, little volcanoes form, and the surface of the mixture appears to be separating, about 10 minutes. I know this description sounds odd—what is happening is hard to describe, but you'll understand when you see it. The liquid is two different shades of white at this point, pure white and a light cream color. Some of the volcanoes can be very large, so be prepared. At the end of the 10 minutes remove from the heat. Stir in the cane syrup and the coconut.

Transfer the sauce to a bowl or large measuring cup (big enough to hold the 5 cups) and place it in a larger bowl filled with ice water to cool quickly. When it reaches 80° place in a blender with the butter and process at medium speed until the butter melts and is incorporated into the sauce, about 30 seconds.

MAKE THE TOPPING Gently combine the mixed fruit.

To serve, place 1 piece of cake in a custard cup and spoon ¼ cup of the sauce over the top. Decorate with 2 tablespoons of the mixed fresh fruit and garnish with a mint sprig, if desired.

Mixed Berry Cobbler

MAKES 10 TO 12 SERVINGS

Who can resist a cobbler, hot from the oven, and brimming with the freshest, most perfect berries at the market? Not I, especially when it's made with an out-of-the ordinary, peppery-sweet dough. The ground chiles give it a gorgeous terra cotta color as well as a flavor you won't find in Granny's recipe. You can use 5 cups of whatever berries are fresh and gorgeous when you shop. Put some whipped cream on that dude, or top it with ice cream, perhaps cinnamon flavored, and sliced fresh strawberries.

2 cups fresh blueberries
2 cups fresh strawberries, stemmed and quartered
1 cup fresh raspberries
2 small fresh apricots, or 1 small fresh peach, peeled, pitted, and thinly sliced
1¼ cups sugar, in all
2 tablespoons vanilla, in all
2 cups all-purpose flour
1 teaspoon ground dried Anaheim chile peppers (see pages 1 and 2)

1 teaspoon ground dried New Mexico chile peppers (see pages 1 and 2)
½ teaspoon ground dried árbol chile peppers (see pages 1 and 2)
½ teaspoon ground cinnamon
1 teaspoon cream of tartar
2 teaspoons baking soda
8 tablespoons (1 stick) unsalted butter, melted
½ cup unflavored yogurt (see page 3)
1¼ cups milk

Preheat the oven to 350°

Combine the blueberries, strawberries, raspberries, and sliced apricots or peach in a 9-inch by 13-inch casserole dish or baking pan. Sprinkle ½ cup of the sugar evenly over the berries, then sprinkle 1 tablespoon of the vanilla over them.

In a food processor place the remaining ¾ cup of the sugar, the flour, dried ground chiles, cinnamon, cream of tartar, and the baking soda. Process just until the dry ingredients are combined, about 30 seconds. Add the remaining 1 tablespoon of the vanilla, the butter, yogurt, and milk, and process just until all the ingredients are thoroughly combined to make a batter. For the best texture, be careful not to overmix. Spread the batter evenly over the berries and bake until the top is browned and firm, about 30 minutes. Serve hot or at room temperature.

Chocolate-Filled Beignets

MAKES 12 BEIGNETS

Unlike the square doughnuts in New Orleans' French Market, these beignets are round, and they each hold a surprise—a rich candy circle made from three delicious flavors of chocolate! If you don't have cookie cutters in the sizes called for, you can use glasses or jars, provided the "cutting edges" aren't too thick. As you read the recipe, you'll see it's a little bit of trouble, but definitely worth it—feed somebody you love with these wonderful chocolate-filled beignets. Ces sont bons!

This is two recipes in one, because you can use the chocolate mixture and the dough to make other treats. Try the chocolate as a dip for fresh fruit—we've tasted it with strawberries with great results—or as a topping for plain cake or ice cream. Just don't refrigerate it so it will stay soft. And use your imagination to come up with other wonderful fillings for the beignets—fresh fruit such as diced apples or bananas, chopped nuts, brown sugar and cinnamon, and so forth. If you have company you could set out bowls of fillings and let your guests make and cook their own—just keep the dough very cold and slip the finished beignets into the freezer for a few minutes to re-chill before frying. I love it when you use my recipes as a springboard for your own kitchen expeditions!

6 tablespoons unsalted butter, cut into 12 pieces
½ ounce semi-sweet chocolate
2½ ounces white chocolate (see page 172)
3 ounces milk chocolate
3¼ cups all-purpose flour, plus flour for dusting
3 tablespoons baking powder

¼ cup sugar, plus 1 tablespoon, in all
1½ teaspoons salt
2 teaspoons vanilla extract
1 cup plus 2 tablespoons milk
2 tablespoons vegetable oil, plus additional oil for frying
2 large eggs, in all
Powdered sugar, optional, or cane syrup (see page 165), optional

Add enough water to the bottom of a double boiler to fill it one-third, place it over high heat, and bring the water to a boil. Place the butter and all the varieties of chocolate in the top of the double boiler over the boiling water, and heat, stirring constantly, just until the butter-chocolate mixture melts. If you don't have a double boiler, you can melt the butter and chocolates in a skillet that will fit atop a 3-quart saucepan one-third full of boiling water. The important thing here is to heat the chocolate just until it melts, but no longer, and to keep stirring constantly as it melts so it will incorporate the butter. Remove the pan of chocolate mixture from the heat and let it cool, stirring every 3 or 4 minutes, until it reaches room temperature.

Place a 12-inch by 12-inch piece of parchment or wax paper on a sheet pan and fold up the sides to form a 6-inch by 6-inch square box. Spread the chocolate mixture evenly inside the paper box—it should be about ½ inch thick—and place in the freezer for at least 30 minutes to harden the chocolate so you can cut it easily.

In the bowl of an electric mixer equipped with a dough hook, combine the flour, baking powder, ¼ cup of the sugar, and the salt. Mix at low speed just until the dry ingredients are combined, then add the vanilla, milk, 2 tablespoons oil, and 1 egg. Mix at low speed until the ingredients are combined, then increase the speed to medium and mix, stopping the mixer occasionally to scrape down the sides of the bowl as necessary, until the ingredients form a soft dough, about 4 minutes. Refrigerate the dough until very cold, at least 3 hours.

When the dough is very cold, make an egg wash by processing in a blender the remaining egg, two tablespoons of water, and the remaining sugar.

Lightly flour a flat surface and transfer the dough to this surface. Lightly flour the dough and a rolling pin and roll out the dough into a rectangle about ¼ inch thick. Using a 2½-inch cookie cutter, cut out 12 circles, and make 12 circles with a 3-inch cookie cutter—do your rolling and cutting in batches if your work surface is small. Brush one side of each dough circle with the egg wash and place them in the refrigerator.

Remove the chocolate from the freezer and, using a 1½-inch cookie cutter, cut 12 circles out of the chocolate, and use a flat spatula to remove them from the parchment or wax paper. Assemble the beignets—place a 3-inch dough circle on a clean surface, egg washed side up, and place a chocolate circle in the center of the dough circle. Center a 2½-inch dough circle, egg washed side down, on top of the chocolate. Bring up the edge of the bottom dough circle over the edge of the top dough circle and seal the edges firmly by crimping them with your fingers or the tines of a fork all the way around. Turn the beignet over and seal the edges again. If you use a fork, flour it occasionally as you work and be careful not to pierce the dough. *This step is very important—you must be sure the seal is tight, or the chocolate will escape from the dough circles and ruin the oil.* Repeat to make 12 beignets, and refrigerate until they are very cold, at least 3 hours.

When you're ready to fry the beignets, pour enough oil into a large skillet with high sides to measure 2 inches, and heat it to 300°. Use a cooking thermometer and adjust the heat so the temperature of the oil stays between 250° and 300°. An electric skillet, if you have one, works great. *Warning: You will notice that as soon as you put the beignets into the oil, the temperature will rapidly increase. You'd think the oil would cool somewhat since the beignets are cold, but the reverse happens—it's a law of thermodynamics and always happens when you add something very cold to something very hot. Watch the temperature closely and be ready to adjust it, because after the rapid rise in temperature, it will fall very rapidly. You don't want it to fall below 250°, yet the beignets may break open and ruin the batch if the oil temperature climbs too high. Also, if the oil is too hot the beignets will brown before they are done on the inside.* Fry the beignets, in batches if necessary to prevent crowding, turning several times, until they are light gold, about 3 to 4 minutes per batch. Drain on paper towels and serve as soon as they are cool enough to handle. Dust lightly with powdered sugar or drizzle with cane syrup, if desired.

Glossary

Andouille (pronounced "ahn-DOO-ee") is a highly-seasoned smoked pork sausage made in Louisiana. Substitute the best quality smoked pork sausage if you cannot find genuine andouille in your area. See page 2 for mail order information.

Appaloosa beans are as speckled—brown and tan—as the horse breed for which they're named. They have a granular, woody texture and a mild, earthy taste, and are popular in soups and tossed with pasta, as well as in Southwestern dishes. When cooked they double their dry size.

Banana peppers, also called Hungarian or wax peppers, are usually so mild that we really shouldn't call them chile peppers at all, although some can range up to medium-hot, so be sure to taste yours before using. They range from yellow to yellow-green to light green in color, and are about 3 to 5 inches long, with a width that tapers from about 1½ inches at the stem end to a gentle point.

Buckwheat flour is made from the seeds of an herb, not a true cereal. Its earthy, assertive flavor is welcome in pancakes, waffles, and baked goods. If you can't find it in your supermarket, it likely will be available in health food stores.

Butterscotch beans, also known as Steuben Yellow Eye, have been known since the 17th century, and may be the original variety used in Boston baked beans. Their texture is firm and their taste is similar to baby red potatoes.

Cane syrup is made by simmering pure sugar cane juice until it reaches the desired dark, rich color and taste. Very sweet, it's traditionally used on pancakes and waffles in the South instead of maple syrup.

Cane vinegar See vinegar.

Cassava See yucca.

Celeriac See celery root.

Celery root, sometimes known under the appropriate names of celeriac or celery knob, is indeed the knobby root of a variety of celery grown especially for this root. By the time you buy it in the store, its stalks and leaves will likely have been snipped off. Celery root can be eaten raw or cooked in a variety of ways, but because it tends to discolor when cut, add a little lemon juice to the salad or cooking water.

Chile peppers (fresh)

Bird, bird's eye, and Thai all refer to the same variety of chile pepper, one that is tiny—no more than 1½ inches long and ¼ inch in diameter. It may be small but it's potent! It's used when bright red and ripe, and also when still green.

Jalapeños are one of the most readily available and popular of all chile peppers—you know, the ones that are sliced and placed on top of nachos at the football stadium. They're smooth-skinned, usually green but ripen to a light, bright red, and are easily seeded and de-veined. They average about 2 inches long and just under 1 inch in diameter. They range from hot to *really* hot.

Poblano peppers are usually mild, but sometimes can have a little heat, so taste to be sure. They are a dark, bright green color, have a rather leathery skin, and generally are 5 to 8 inches in length, although there is a miniature version available in some markets. They taper, in an uneven, convoluted fashion, from a diameter of about 1½ inches at the stem end to a rounded point.

Serrano peppers, which ripen from green to red to yellow, are very hot in spite of their small size, only about 1½ inches long.

Chinese 5-Spice Powder is a blend of ground cinnamon, cloves, fennel seeds, star anise, and peppercorns. You can buy jars already mixed, or for best results combine your own in the proportion that works for you.

Chocolate, white See white chocolate.

Cilantro, also called Chinese parsley, is the leaf of the coriander plant, and has a pungent flavor highly prized by cooks in Asia and Latin America. Although cilantro looks very much like flat parsley, the taste is so different that the two are not interchangeable.

Coconut milk in cans is available in the international sections of supermarkets, or in Asian or Latin American markets. We always use unsweetened (the sweetened varieties are used for drinks like piña collada), and the brands we use most often are Chaokoh and Aroy-D, which are products of Thailand.

Corn flour is simply corn meal that has been milled longer to produce the fine texture. It's often available in the same section as corn meal and specialty flours, but if you can't find it, several brands of "fish fry" are actually corn flour—just be sure it's unseasoned.

Creole mustard, which is a soft brownish-golden color rather than the vivid spread baseball fans slather over hot dogs, is made by grinding brown mustard seeds, then soaking the paste with vinegar and spices. You can actually see the specks of the seeds.

Fennel is a very useful, fragrant plant with a very light green bulb and stems that resemble celery, and feathery, brilliant green "leaves." The bulb and stems may be eaten raw or cooked, and the foliage can be used raw as garnish or added during the last minutes of cooking for a delicate touch of sweet flavor slightly reminiscent of anise. This variety is called Florence fennel or finocchio. It is from another variety, common fennel, that the seeds we use in our recipes are harvested. You may be able to find fennel seeds already ground, or buy them whole and grind them yourself in a coffee grinder.

Fenugreek seeds may be purchased whole or ground; if you can find only whole, grind them yourself in a coffee grinder. With a distinctive flavor somewhere between bitter and sweet, fenugreek is a common ingredient in curry mixes. Fenugreek is unlike anything else, so once you've experienced it, you'll never mistake it for another seasoning. If you can't find it in the spice section of your market, try the tea section.

Filo See phyllo.

"Gills" of mushrooms are the name for the spongy convolutions that range out from the stem on the mushroom's underside. They're usually a little darker than the top portion.

Granulated brown sugar, which is also called "Brownulated," is just what its name says—brown sugar that is granulated rather than soft.

Jicama (HEE-cah-mah) is a brownish gray vegetable with a crisp, off-white flesh which can be eaten either cooked or raw. Popular in Mexico.

Kirschwasser is a clear, colorless unsweetened brandy, generally 80 to 100 proof (40% to 50% alcohol by volume) that in this country is not usually consumed alone, but used to flavor cakes and pastries and the famous Cherries Jubilee. Literally translated from the German, it means "cherry water," for it's distilled from cherries and their pits.

Kohlrabi is a member of the turnip family, and, not surprisingly, tastes a little like its cousin, only a bit milder and sweeter. Both the bulb and leaves are edible; I've added diced kohlrabi bulb to several of my recipes because I like the distinctive flavor and crisp texture it adds. Both the green and purple varieties are delicious and work equally well.

Lemon grass is a reed whose fragrance and taste are surprisingly lemon-like. It is used for flavoring foods by adding lengths during cooking then removing them, or grinding it so fine that its rather dry texture will not be apparent. The coarse outer leaves are light yellow-green, while the more tender inner leaves are very pale green. Lemon grass has long been a favorite with Asian, especially Thai, cooks, and now that it's more readily available in supermarkets, the rest of us can enjoy it as well. If you absolutely can't find lemon grass, substitute fresh lemon balm, an herb with lemon-scented leaves.

Mangoes were once known only in the tropics, but now have gained wide acceptance for their delicious flavor and attractive appearance. The skin of a fully ripe mango is yellow, sometimes touched with red, and its juicy flesh is bright yellow-orange. Generally ovoid in shape, mangoes have a single, unusually large seed which clings tenaciously to the flesh, necessitating a very sharp knife. A few people's skin is sensitive to the enzymes in mangoes, so if you think yours might be, just wear latex or vinyl gloves when handling them. If your market stocks more than one variety, use whichever looks best, for they're all very similar.

To peel and chop a mango, place it on the counter with the stem end up and the more narrow side facing you. With a sharp knife, slice from top to bottom about ½ inch away from the center of the fruit, then turn the mango and make another slice about ½ inch away from the center of the fruit on the other side. Now take the two pieces you've sliced away and make cuts, about ½ inch apart, in both directions, from the cut surface all the way to the skin of each piece. *You can see such a sectioned mango piece in photograph No. 10, Bronzed Trout with Spinach-Mango Purée.* To loosen the pieces of fruit, push the skin toward the fruit, as though you were going to turn it inside-out. Now you can gently scrape the pieces off the skin with a spoon.

Masa harina is a Mexican-style flour made from ground, dehydrated, whole-kernel corn which has been treated with lime. It is used to make tortillas, tamales and some baked goods. Masa harina may be enriched with various vitamins.

Mirliton is a vegetable that has many names, and is popular in numerous cultures. It's also called vegetable pear in New Orleans, chayote in Latin America, and christophene in France, the French Caribbean, and parts of Africa. The mirliton has bland, very pale green flesh inside the rough light green skin. It's wonderful grated raw into salads, diced into stews, or split and stuffed with well-seasoned seafood or ham mixed with vegetables. I like to use it because it readily takes on the flavor of the other foods that surround it. It grows on vines, and is so prolific in our sub-tropical climate that gardeners and cooks are constantly coming up with new ways to prepare it.

Mushrooms are important in many of these recipes, and I like to use various types. One of my favorites is *portobello*, which basically is just an overgrown white mushroom. They can be as large as 6 inches in diameter, and are so meaty that some vegetarian restaurants grill them and use in place of meat in sandwiches or as a main course. I think their taste is great, and they're also perfect for stuffing. *Shiitake* mushrooms are slightly curled, generally creamy-brown in color, and measure about 2 or 3 inches. Cultivated *enoki* mushrooms are easily recognizable by their long, slender stems topped with tiny round caps. Their texture is crisp and delicate, and their flavor mild and more fruity than woodsy.

When a recipe calls for "mushrooms" without listing a variety, use whatever are fresh at your market. And when unusual mushrooms are available, experiment with them, and get to know the variety of textures and flavors out there. There are conflicting views on whether or not to wash mushrooms. They ought to be cleaned, but as they are composed primarily of water, if you wash them they'll take on even more water, so a good but gentle brushing is probably your best bet. Culinary specialty shops sell special mushroom brushes—they're very soft but do a great job.

Mustard, Creole See Creole mustard.

Papaya is a popular tropical fruit available nearly country-wide in supermarkets and specialty produce shops. It's usually fairly ovoid in shape, with fragrant golden flesh and lots of shiny black seeds inside a golden skin. Easy to peel and chop, it's used in several of our recipes, and is wonderful sliced, perhaps sprinkled with fresh lime juice. A very few individuals have skin that is sensitive to its enzymes, so if you are one of these, protect your hands with gloves while you handle it.

Parsnips look like long white carrots, and their texture is very similar. Their flavor is sharper, though, reminiscent of turnips, but often sweet if harvested in the fall or early winter. An excellent source of vitamin C, parsnips have not gotten the respect they're due, for they can be prepared in many different ways, including simple boiling and mashing like potatoes, poaching, and roasting.

Phyllo is the Greek word for "leaf," and the pastry is comprised of very thin layers that puff when baked. If you've ever had baklava, you've had phyllo pastry dough. We've used it to wrap some of our seasoned meat and seafood fillings, then fried the rolls, which makes the dough crisp, flaky and golden brown. It's also correctly spelled "filo," and pronounced FEE-low. Available frozen or fresh in most supermarkets, it should be kept closed until ready to use, and covered with a layer of plastic wrap then damp paper towels while working, as it needs to stay moist for best results.

Radicchio leaves look like small, purplish-red cabbage leaves. A member of the chicory family, radicchio is native to and popular in northern Italy, and is widely available all year. Its sharp, slightly bitter taste adds a nice jolt to salads and its lovely color makes it great as a garnish. Just be sure the leaves are crisp and unbroken.

Rice is one of the official state foods of Louisiana! We could write a whole book on rice—in fact it's been done—but of course we don't have quite that much space here. The most important thing for me to tell you is that when we specify "rice," we mean processed or previously washed rice.

If you don't use processed rice, you should wash it to remove the excess starch so it won't be sticky after it's cooked, and here's how. Place the measured uncooked rice in a bowl or saucepan with enough water to cover it. Fill your hands with rice and move your hands back and forth in the water several times, then release that rice and grab another hand-full, repeating until all the rice has been washed. Drain off the water, add more, and continue washing a total of four times. The water should then be almost clear—the cloudiness in the water was the excess starch.

Basmati rice has less moisture content than regular rice, as well as a slightly nutlike flavor and aroma, and goes well with Indian and Middle Eastern dishes. Sometimes we *want* the rice to be sticky; in that case we specify *long-grain* rice, and suggest *Mahatma®* brand. Brown rice is just white rice, still wearing its natural brown coating on each grain.

Rice wine is a sweet wine made from fermenting glutinous rice, generally with a low alcohol content. It can be used in any recipe that calls for vinegar, either to replace the vinegar completely, or in combination with the vinegar. Warmed, it makes a very soothing toddy. The best known, sake and mirin, are from Japan, but the Chinese also brew several varieties. Be sure you buy a non-salted variety.

Rutabaga looks like a large turnip, and botanically speaking, it may be a cross between a turnip and a cabbage. Its yellow-orange flesh is great cooked any one of a dozen ways, and although its wonderful sweet flavor is distinctive, it mixes well with other vegetables. It's particularly popular in Scandinavia, and in fact some people call it "Swedish turnip."

Star anise is similar to anise, in that both have a licorice flavor, but star anise has a slightly more bitter flavor than the sweeter anise. Although both flavorings are used in Asian cuisine, Chinese cooks are more likely to use star anise, and in fact it's one of the ingredients of Chinese 5-Spice Powder. Anise and star anise come from different plants families. I much prefer the cleaner, less pungent flavor of star anise over anise seeds.

Sweet Rice Wine See Rice Wine.

Sweetened condensed milk is used in one or two of these recipes; the brand we use is Borden's®.

Tamari is a variety of soy sauce, but aged longer than usual for a rich, complex flavor and a thicker consistency that holds up well in cooking. There is considerable variation among brands of tamari; nothing but soy should be used in the processing. Taste them, and use the one you like best.

Tasso is a highly seasoned, air-dried Cajun ham. If it is not available in your area, substitute well-smoked ham, or better yet, see page 2 for mail order information.

Vinegar is another ingredient of which there are numerous varieties.

> **Balsamic** is an Italian vinegar, made from white grape juice, that gets its color from aging in numerous different wooden barrels over the years.

> **White balsamic** is a blend of white wine vinegar and the boiled-down musts of white grapes. It is lighter in color and less intense than its cousin, the darker balsamic vinegar.

> **Wine vinegar**, just like wines, comes in red or white, and they add a rich or light touch according to the type. All the above vinegars should be easy to find in supermarkets or specialty markets.

> **Cane vinegar,** a Louisiana product, is becoming more widely available because it's so good! It's made from sugar cane juice, as is molasses, and adds a distinctive sweetness to the acidity you expect from vinegar. If you absolutely can't find it where you shop, substitute the same amount of apple cider vinegar plus 1 tablespoon of cane syrup. Or for mail order, write to C. S. Steen Syrup Mill, Inc., P. O. Box 339, Abbeville LA 70510.

White chocolate isn't really chocolate at all, but "classic white confection," according to the label on the Ghirardelli® brand (and experts at their main office), one of the good quality products we recommend, along with Lindt® and Tobler®. It does contain cocoa butter, however, to give it the rich flavor we expect, plus vanilla and sugar, and perhaps a bit of the residual chocolate solid might remain in the cocoa butter (chocolate fat) after processing.

Yucca, a root with a rough brown skin and white, crisp flesh, is also known as cassava or manioc. It can be a foot long and 3 or 4 inches in diameter, and is so hard that you'll need a sharp, thin knife to cut it. Originally from South America, yucca root is available year-round in Caribbean and Latin American markets, and many supermarkets. It also is used to make tapioca.

INDEX